MW01644958

40 Days of
FOCUS

Prayer, Fasting, & Revival

© 2024. Central Florida Baptist Association. All Rights Reserved.
No part of this publication may be reproduced, stored in a retrieval system, or transmitted in any form by any means, electronic, mechanical, photocopying, recording, or otherwise, except brief extracts for the purpose of review, without written permission from the copyright owner.

Editing, Layout, and Cover Design by Sheila R. (Boyd) Morgan, EdD, sheilaraemorgan@gmail.com, www.sheilaraeboyd.com.

Scripture quotations marked **(KJV)** have been taken from the King James Version Bible, public domain.

Scripture quotations marked **(NKJV)** have been taken from the New King James Version®. Copyright © 1982 by Thomas Nelson. Used by permission. All rights reserved.

Scripture quotations marked **(CSB)** have been taken from the Christian Standard Bible®, Copyright © 2017 by Holman Bible Publishers. Used by permission. Christian Standard Bible® and CSB® are federally registered trademarks of Holman Bible Publishers.

Scripture quotations marked **(ESV)** are from The ESV® Bible (The Holy Bible, English Standard Version®), © 2001 by Crossway, a publishing ministry of Good News Publishers. Used by permission. All rights reserved.
Scripture texts marked (NASB®) are taken from the New American Standard Bible®, Copyright ©1995 by The Lockman Foundation. Used by permission. All rights reserved. lockman.org.

Scripture quotations marked **(NLT)** are taken from the *Holy Bible*, New Living Translation, copyright ©1996, 2004, 2015 by Tyndale House Foundation. Used by permission of Tyndale House Publishers, Carol Stream, Illinois 60188. All rights reserved.

Scripture quotations marked **(NIV)** are taken from the Holy Bible, New International Version®, NIV®. Copyright © 1973, 1978, 1984, 2011 by Biblica, Inc.™ Used by permission of Zondervan. All rights reserved worldwide. www.zondervan.com. The "NIV" and "New International Version" are trademarks registered in the United States Patent and Trademark Office by Biblica, Inc.™

Disclaimer: Before embarking on any fasting regimen, it is important to consult with a medical professional. The information provided in this book is for educational purposes only and should not be considered medical advice. The authors and the Central Florida Baptist Association are not responsible for any consequences resulting from the use or misuse of the information provided.

Written by a group of pastors of the Central Florida Baptist Association, *40 Days of Focus: Prayer, Fasting, & Revival* is a collection of short devotionals with a focus on prayer, fasting, and revival. Rather than presenting a theological commentary, the devotionals are presented as a practical guide that will help you grow in your walk with Christ. It is these pastors' prayer that over the next 40 days, the devotionals will help you experience a renewed desire for seeking the presence of God.

TABLE OF CONTENTS

AN INTRODUCTION TO PRAYER

Dr. Lanelle Pickett, Sr.
Good Hope Missionary Baptist Church of Bartow, Florida

"Rejoice evermore. Pray without ceasing."
1 Thessalonians 5:16-17 (NKJV)

Paul reminds believers to "Rejoice evermore" and to "Pray without ceasing."

Some might ask, "What is prayer?" To be sure, a Google search will yield countless definitions. Theologians, philosophers, scholars, and academicians will all offer impressive discourses and dialogues on prayer. However, one of the precise interpretations of the word, "prayer," is simply "speaking to God and God speaking back to us." I confess God has not spoken to me in an audible voice as He did to Moses, Joshua, and Samuel. However, He has spoken to my heart and mind in prayer.

When you study the life of Jesus, you find that He had an amazing prayer life. He prayed early in the morning, alone, and with others. He taught His disciples to pray. He prayed as He agonized in the Garden of Gethsemane. Jesus even prayed while dying on Calvary's cross.

Imagine having an open invitation to speak with any president, king, emperor, or prime minister of your choosing. More importantly, imagine that such a powerful ruler was not only eager to hear from you regularly but *expecting* to hear from you on a frequent basis. You may think that would really be great.

However, here's a reality that's far greater: as a believer in Jesus Christ, you have the distinct honor, privilege, and pleasure of having an audience with the King of Kings and Lord of Lords! You don't need an appointment; there's no bureaucracy, no red tape, no fees . . . and you don't have to wait in line! That's the beauty of prayer, and it's your privilege! What a joyous privilege we have as believers in Jesus Christ to pray. Remember, prayer is a privilege; so, let's use it often and enjoy the sweet fellowship with our awesome God!

In the hymn entitled "What a Friend We Have in Jesus," Joseph Medlicott Scriven wrote,

> "What a friend we have in Jesus,
> All our sins and griefs to bear!
> What a privilege to carry
> Everything to God in prayer."

Journal

AN INTRODUCTION TO FASTING

Dr. Matt McCraw
First Baptist Church of Bartow, Florida

When you hear the word, "fasting," what comes to mind? Perhaps you think, "I'm not exactly sure what that is." Perhaps you say to yourself, "Well, that's just not for me." Maybe you even go so far as to say, "Fasting is for those religious zealots." Of all the spiritual disciplines, fasting may be the one that escapes most Christians. Why is that the case? Perhaps the scarcity of Christian fasting is because many Christians don't properly understand it.

Donald Whitney says in his book, *Spiritual Disciplines for the Christian Life*, "Christian fasting is a believer's voluntary abstinence from food for spiritual purposes." Tim Challies clarifies further by saying, "In fasting you are withholding from yourself something you need (food) in order to pursue something you need even more (communion with God)" (challies.com). That's the heart of fasting: voluntarily giving up something in order to gain something greater.

As we think of fasting, let's reflect on three truths regarding it:

First, fasting should be *practiced*. The practice of fasting has taken an unhealthy shift in recent years. Not only are many Christians rarely (or never) practicing the spiritual act of fasting, some are also altering the nature of fasting. We must remember that fasting is about giving up food to focus on hearing and experiencing God. Fasting is not about giving up Facebook, music, television, gossip, gambling, or other trivial things. Fasting is giving up *food*.

To be clear, it may be helpful and good for you to give up things other than food. Most people spend too much time on social media and would benefit from spending less time on there. It is certainly good for our souls to give up habitual sins that plague our lives. However, giving up such things should be considered the general pursuit of godliness and sanctification. It's good . . . but it's not fasting.

How do we know this reality to be true? How do we know that fasting is about giving up food rather than giving up something else? First, remember that giving up food is giving up something that we *need*. We don't need Facebook. We can certainly live without television. It may do you well to give up such things. We definitely don't need sin in our lives. However, we do need food. God has so designed us that we cannot live if we continually give up food.

The second way we know that fasting is about food is because we have multiple biblical examples of fasting in the Scriptures. Repeatedly, these examples are of people willingly giving up food for a period of time. Consider when Moses

"fell down . . . in the presence of the Lord for forty days and forty nights. [He] did not eat food or drink water . . .."
Deuteronomy 9:18 (CSB)

Matthew 4:2 speaks of Jesus' fast. It says,

"After he had fasted forty days and forty nights, he was hungry."
Matthew 4:2 (CSB)

Why was Jesus hungry? Because he fasted from food. So, fasting is about giving up food.

A natural question might follow: does fasting mean that I have to give up *all* food? Generally speaking, the answer is yes. However, there are different types of fasts that Christians may choose to practice depending on the situation. A regular fast is when someone chooses to fast from all food or drink except for water. A partial fast is when you give up some aspect of food or drink but not all of it. You may choose to give up solid foods but still consume liquids. You may choose to eat only one meal per day. A third type of fasting is a collective fast. This fast is when more than one person (sometimes an entire congregation) commits to fast for a particular reason.

Secondly, not only should fasting be practiced, but it should also be *purposeful*. No matter what type of fasting you practice, you should do so with purposeful intention. Jesus teaches us this reality in Matthew 6:16-18 when he speaks about what we are to do when we fast. We are not to be haphazard in our fasting. We shouldn't simply "wing it" and see what happens. Rather, we should have a purpose behind our fasting. Ultimately, the purpose behind fasting should be nothing less than communion with God. We should want to hear from God and experience Him. Some of the purposes behind our fasting can include strengthening our prayer life; seeking God's guidance; expressing grief; seeking deliverance or protection; expressing repentance; humbling ourselves; expressing a desire to see God work; seeking strength for ministry, to overcome temptation, to express love and worship to God, and more. Whatever our reason, we should be purposeful.

Finally, fasting should be *prayerful*. Fasting and prayer go together like peas and carrots. So often, when we see fasting in the Bible it is accompanied by prayer. For example, we see in Ezra 8:23 that the fasting of the Jewish people was accompanied by prayer:

**"So we fasted and pleaded with our God about this,
and he was receptive to our prayer."
Ezra 8:23 (CSB)**

We see in Acts 13:3 that the early church fasted and prayed:

"Then after they had fasted, prayed,
and laid hands on them, they sent them off."
Acts 13:3 (CSB)

While prayer may be practiced without fasting (after all, we are to pray without ceasing), fasting should not be done without prayer. When we fast, we experience a natural response. We are hungry. We are tired. Perhaps we're even grumpy. The natural response we have to fasting should prompt us to supernatural action: prayer.

Prayer is a supernatural act by which we speak to the God of the universe. Prayer is miraculous. If your fasting is not accompanied by prayer, if your fasting is not intentionally seeking communion with God, then you simply have a bad diet plan.

Why do we fast? We fast because we need God. Fasting helps remind us of that reality. Fasting is an intentional pursuit of the presence of God. It is our effort coupled with God's empowerment. We don't fast to earn God's favor or try to impress Him. Rather, we fast because we have already received God's favor through the work of Jesus and because we have been impressed by His great love for us. We want more of Him and His presence in our lives. Fasting magnifies our dependence on God.

Therefore, fasting should be practiced in your life; your fasting should be purposeful; and your fasting should be prayerful. Do not neglect this incredible opportunity to experience the presence of God.

Journal

AN INTRODUCTION TO REVIVAL

Pastor Matt Ellis
First Baptist Church of Polk City, Florida

A large crowd had gathered for a momentous occasion. Most of them had only recently breathed the air of freedom. About 50 years earlier, Solomon's glorious Temple had been ransacked and demolished, and most of the Israelites had been taken captive by the Babylonians. However, they were now free and back in Jerusalem. The two-year project to build the foundation for the second Temple had been completed, and God's people wanted to celebrate this event with a time of praise and thanksgiving. They had gathered, craving an occasion to celebrate and hope again.

However, it was not merely a time of joy. Some of the crowd celebrated, as would be expected . . . but others grieved and wept.

"But many of the older priests, Levites, and family heads, who had seen the first temple, wept loudly when they saw the foundation of this temple, but many others shouted joyfully."
Ezra 3:12 (CSB)

Why were the older folks weeping? Because they had seen the glory of Solomon's Temple 50 years earlier. When they looked at the foundation of this second Temple, they knew it would pale in comparison; and the only appropriate response was to weep.

Why were the younger folks celebrating? Because the current, inferior Temple was all they knew. They couldn't imagine anything better than their current experience.

There are similarities when we speak of revival. There are folks in our midst who have never experienced the glory of God in a time of revival, either privately or corporately. So, they may find joy in religious experiences that are far from what God desires.

However, some Christians are rightfully sad. They have studied God's Word to see the happiness that can be had in Him, and they have experienced the glory of God in their own lives. When they look around at the current state of so many spiritually lethargic churches and Christians, the only appropriate response is to grieve. Like the older folks in the book of Ezra, they weep because they know there is something so much better.

So, let's not merely talk about revival as something in the past. Let's pray and expectantly work toward a time of spiritual renewal and refreshment in our day.

To begin, we need at least a working definition of revival. Revival is simply "a season of time when God awakens His people to despise their sins, receive His forgiveness and cleansing, and enjoy Him." Out of that soul-satisfying love relationship that brings them great fulfillment, God's people are motivated and empowered by His Holy Spirit to serve Him in Kingdom work generally with greater effectiveness.

Now, let's unpack that definition by looking at Isaiah 6. While every personal and corporate season of revival is different, Isaiah 6 reveals the typical path many revivals tend to follow. It is a journey with five basic phases. Let's consider each of them:

1. I must realize my need for the Lord.

"In the year that King Uzziah died, I saw the Lord seated on a high and lofty throne, and the hem of his robe filled the temple."
Isaiah 6:1 (CSB)

As this chapter begins, we enter a funeral parlor. Someone has died. King Uzziah had been a great king who enabled his people to prosper in many ways. On top of all his accomplishments, he lived to please the Lord and led his people to do the same. However, as he grew older, he became proud. He became self-sufficient . . . and with that sinful heart attitude, he overstepped his bounds with the priests; and it led to his ruin. The Lord gave him leprosy, and he died.

This created a great degree of uncertainty. Would the next king lead so that the people of his nation could prosper, or would they suffer because of his poor or self-serving leadership? Would he follow the Lord or lead God's people away from Him?

This sort of tension is typically what begins a revival journey. Life gets hard, and we aren't sure how things will pan out. However, uncertainty and pain are often good because they motivate us to seek a solution. A season of revival may be just around the corner.

2. I must reflect on who the Lord is.

"In the year that King Uzziah died, I saw the Lord seated on a high and lofty throne, and the hem of his robe filled the temple. Seraphim were standing above him; they each had six wings: with two they covered their faces, with two they covered their feet, and with two they flew.
And one called to another:
Holy, holy, holy is the LORD of Armies; his glory fills the whole earth.
The foundations of the doorways shook at the sound of their voices,
and the temple was filled with smoke."
Isaiah 6:1-4 (CSB)

In Isaiah's desperation and fear, the Lord revealed Himself. It is noteworthy that the one attribute of God that came across most clearly to Isaiah was the Lord's holiness.

What does it mean that God is holy? At its very essence it means that God is set apart from everything else. There is nothing and no one like Him. There is no duplicity in Him. His beauty is in His purity. It's not merely that He has never sinned; His beauty is in His perfect righteousness. There is absolutely nothing and no one so glorious as He!

People who experience times of personal or corporate revival typically say that they came into a greater understanding and experience of God's holiness. They also realize that God's holiness is not merely an attribute; it is the beauty of God that causes their hearts to stand in awe of Him. They even sometimes say that they understand more clearly what it means to have an appropriate "fear of the Lord."

3. I must acknowledge my sinfulness and repent.

"Then I said: Woe is me for I am ruined because I am a man of unclean lips and live among a people of unclean lips, and because my eyes have seen the King, the Lord of Armies."
Isaiah 6:5 (CSB)

After God graciously allowed Isaiah to experience His holiness, the prophet looked back at himself and couldn't help but bemoan his sinfulness. In a place of spiritual darkness, Isaiah's sin and the sin of his peers weren't so visible. However, the dirt of sin could not be hidden in the light of God's presence and holiness. It was only appropriate for Isaiah to acknowledge and weep over his sinfulness.

So often we feel pleased at the spiritual condition of our hearts. That's because the spiritual light is off. When God enables us to experience the light of His holiness, we realize just how utterly sinful we really are. Sins that we thought were small and insignificant become massive in our eyes. Unresolved sins are brought to mind. Sins hidden away in the closets of our minds begin to put off a putrid aroma.

While this time of profound conviction may seem unpleasant (and it is!), it allows us the opportunity to do a deep spiritual cleaning. I discovered in my own experience during a time of revival that I absolutely loved finding unconfessed sin because I enjoyed the experience of owning it and receiving God's forgiveness and cleansing.

This brings up a very important revival principle: the irony of revival is that we have to go down before we can go up. We must go down in repentance before we can go up in restoration and joy! And the deeper we go in genuine brokenness and repentance, the higher we can go in happiness in our God.

4. I must receive the Lord's forgiveness.

"Then one of the seraphim flew to me, and in his hand was a glowing coal
that he had taken from the altar with tongs.
He touched my mouth with it and said:
Now that this has touched your lips, your iniquity is removed
and your sin is atoned for."
Isaiah 6:6-7 (CSB)

After Isaiah acknowledged his sin and expressed genuine grief over it, we read that an angel grabbed a red-hot coal with tongs and placed it on Isaiah's lips. Do you think it hurt Isaiah? Of course, it did! It hurt badly! And this pictures the pain that is sometimes required to make things right.

So many people would love to have a clear conscience, but they aren't willing to go through what is necessary to get that clean conscience. Sometimes it requires that we humble ourselves and then go to someone and apologize for our words or behavior. Sometimes getting cleaned up demands that we acknowledge something we did wrong . . . even if it means going to the authorities.

We would all love to simply get God's forgiveness and then forget what we did. We don't want consequences. However, there are times when we can only obtain true freedom when we own what we did and make the appropriate amends, if necessary.

Even if getting spiritually clean before God doesn't require anything overtly painful for us, it certainly caused pain for our Lord and Savior, Jesus Christ. He bore our sin and received God's punishment for it on the cross. We can be forgiven, and it's free—but it was certainly not cheap.

5. I must engage in service to the Lord.

"Then I heard the voice of the Lord asking:
'Who will I send? Who will go for us?' I said: 'Here I am. Send me.'
And he replied: 'Go! Say to these people: Keep listening,
but do not understand; keep looking, but do not perceive.
Make the minds of these people dull;
deafen their ears and blind their eyes;
otherwise they might see with their eyes and hear with their ears,
understand with their minds, turn back, and be healed.'
Then I said, 'Until when, Lord?'
And he replied: 'Until cities lie in ruins without inhabitants,
houses are without people, the land is ruined and desolate,
and the Lord drives the people far away,
leaving great emptiness in the land.
Though a tenth will remain in the land, it will be burned again.
Like the terebinth or the oak that leaves a stump when felled,
the holy seed is the stump.'"
Isaiah 6:8-13 (CSB)

So, to quickly rehash the typical revival journey, Isaiah's pain focused his attention on the Lord. The Lord revealed His holiness, leading Isaiah to feel guilty about his sinful condition. Then he went through the painful process of doing what was necessary to receive cleansing and freedom.

So, what's next? Being obedient and serving the Lord. When Isaiah experienced a personal revival, the Lord spoke up and said, "I've got a job that needs done. Do I have any volunteers?"

I can imagine that Isaiah was like a young child in school. He shot his hand in the air and fidgeted wildly to get the Lord's attention. When Isaiah was revived, he naturally craved to serve the Lord. He said, "Here I am! Send me!"

But I want us to notice what the Lord said after Isaiah volunteered. God essentially told the prophet that he was selected for the task of proclaiming truth to the people of Israel . . . but they weren't going to respond positively. Isaiah would serve the Lord but wouldn't see much fruit for his labor.

Friend, if we go through a time of revival and are spiritually renewed, we will want to serve the Lord. We may anticipate that others will jump at the opportunity to enjoy the Lord, too. Sometimes they will . . . but most of the time they won't.

So, this chapter in Isaiah ends where it started. As Isaiah began to serve the Lord, he was in a time of discomfort and uncertainty. These difficulties would give him sufficient motivation to seek the Lord as he began the revival journey all over again.

Don't lose heart, my friend, if the Lord graciously gives you a season of spiritual renewal and then life gets hard. It may simply be the Lord's way of giving you a reason to stay close to Him. Your trials may be a blessing in disguise.

Final Thoughts

As you read the following daily devotions that speak about prayer, fasting, and revival, will you passionately seek the Lord with all your heart? Will you submit to His leadership and do anything He asks of you on a journey to enjoy Him more? Will you obey Him no matter what He tells you to do? I will pray that you do.

Journal

Day 1

STICK TO YOUR FAST BY RESOLVING IT IN YOUR HEART

Pastor Mike Harrell
Fuel Church of Lakeland, Florida

"But Daniel resolved that he would not defile himself with the king's food,
or with the wine that he drank.
Therefore he asked the chief of the eunuchs to allow him
not to defile himself.
And God gave Daniel favor and compassion in the sight of the chief of the
eunuchs, and the chief of the eunuchs said to Daniel,
'I fear my lord the king, who assigned your food and your drink;
for why should he see that you were in worse condition than the youths
who are of your own age?
So you would endanger my head with the king.'
Then Daniel said to the steward whom the chief of the eunuchs had
assigned over Daniel, Hananiah, Mishael, and Azariah,
'Test your servants for ten days;
let us be given vegetables to eat and water to drink.
Then let our appearance and the appearance of the youths
who eat the king's food be observed by you,
and deal with your servants according to what you see.'
So he listened to them in this matter, and tested them for ten days.
At the end of ten days it was seen that they were better in appearance

and fatter in flesh than all the youths who ate the king's food.
So the steward took away their food and the wine they were to drink,
and gave them vegetables."
Daniel 1:8-16 (ESV)

Fasting is a powerful, spiritual discipline that has been practiced by believers for centuries. It involves abstaining from food or other activities for a set period of time to focus on spiritual matters and draw closer to God. When we fast, we demonstrate our dependence on God and our need for His strength and provision. We also seek His will and direction for our lives and surrender our desires and agendas to Him.

At the outset of each fast, determine in your heart that you will complete it. This will give you the resolve you need as the fast progresses. You will be tempted to stop fasting, especially if you are fasting from food. Go ahead and make up your mind that you are going to do this and that nothing will get in your way. If you make this resolve in advance before the temptations start coming, you will be able to withstand the battle for your heart.

Daniel chapter 1 shows us the importance of having a resolved heart:

"But Daniel resolved that he would not defile himself with the king's food,
or with the wine that he drank.
Therefore he asked the chief of the eunuchs
to allow him not to defile himself."
Daniel 1:8 (ESV)

Fasting is never easy no matter how long you have been practicing it. Because fasting and prayer brings you closer to God, there will be opposition both from within and without. At times you may convince yourself that you no longer need to continue even though you have not reached your intended goal. Other times stress and other factors may be at work to drive you off course. No matter the cause, setting your heart with resolve before you begin will help you remain faithful along the way.

Daniel was faithful to remain committed to God no matter what came his way, and the Lord was faithful to Daniel and showed him great favor. This is a valuable lesson for us as we fast. Resolve in your heart now; so when temptation comes, you have already settled the matter.

Action Steps:

1. Set Clear Intentions: Before beginning your fast, take time to set clear intentions and goals for your fast. Write down why you are fasting, what you hope to achieve spiritually, and how you plan to maintain your resolve throughout the fast. Having a clear understanding of your purpose will help you stay focused and committed when faced with challenges.

2. Daily Renewal of Resolve: Each day, take time to renew your resolve and commitment to your fast. Begin each morning with prayer and meditation on your intentions, reaffirming your dedication to honoring God through your fast. Throughout the day, whenever you feel tempted or discouraged, remind yourself of your purpose and of the importance of staying faithful to your commitment. By continuously renewing your resolve, you will strengthen your perseverance and ability to withstand challenges.

Journal

Day 2

FASTING FOR ANSWERED PRAYER

Pastor Mike Harrell
Fuel Church of Lakeland, Florida

There are times when our prayers need to be accompanied by fasting for greater outcomes. Fasting is generally associated with higher devotion and greater intimacy with the Lord, which will always increase the effectiveness of our prayer life. To state it very simply, some things will not happen until we add fasting to our prayer life.

"When they came to the crowd, a man came up to Jesus,
falling on his knees before Him and saying,
'Lord, have mercy on my son, for he is a lunatic and is very ill;
for he often falls into the fire and often into the water. I brought him to Your disciples, and they could not cure him.'
And Jesus answered and said, 'You unbelieving and perverted generation, how long shall I be with you? How long shall I put up with you?
Bring him here to Me.'
And Jesus rebuked him, and the demon came out of him,
and the boy was cured at once.
Then the disciples came to Jesus privately and said,
'Why could we not drive it out?'
And He said to them, 'Because of the littleness of your faith;
for truly I say to you, if you have faith the size of a mustard seed,

you will say to this mountain, "Move from here to there," and it will move; and nothing will be impossible to you. [But this kind does not go out except by prayer and fasting.']"
Matthew 17:14-21 (NASB)

One of our pastors has three children with cystic fibrosis, a genetic disorder affecting the lungs. There is no medical cure at this time for this disease, but I believe our Heavenly Father can do all things. I spent years praying for them, but they remained sick much of the time and simply were not thriving. One year I spent 21 days praying and fasting, asking the Father to heal these beautiful teenagers from this terrible condition. Later that year a new medication came out that has completely changed their lives, and now they are thriving and playing sports. I have no way of knowing whether my prayer and fasting had any impact at all, but I know I did all I could to bring them to the Healer.

Running to God with prayer and fasting doesn't have to be our last resort. When it becomes our first response, we live with the peace that our sovereign Father is working things out.

Action Steps:

1. Evaluate the Need for Fasting: Reflect on areas of your life or specific circumstances where you feel your prayers could benefit from the addition of fasting. Consider situations where you've been praying diligently but have yet to see a breakthrough or where you sense a deeper need for God's intervention. Seek clarity and guidance from the Holy Spirit on whether fasting is appropriate and necessary to enhance the effectiveness of your prayers.

2. Persist in Faith and Expectancy: As you embark on your fast, maintain a posture of faith and expectancy, believing that God will hear and answer your prayers according to His will. Trust in His faithfulness and sovereignty, knowing that He is capable of bringing about miraculous breakthroughs and transformations in your life and circumstances. Stay rooted in the promises of God's Word, meditating on passages like Jeremiah 29:11, which affirm His plans for your welfare and future. Throughout the fast, continue to pray fervently, seeking God's guidance, provision, and favor; and remain open to His leading and direction.

Journal

Day 3

STAY COMMITTED TO YOUR FAST: THE RESULTS ARE WORTH THE SACRIFICE

Pastor Mike Harrell
Fuel Church of Lakeland, Florida

"For I know the plans I have for you, declares the LORD, plans for welfare and not for evil, to give you a future and a hope."
Jeremiah 29:11 (ESV)

By about day three of fasting and prayer, you should be in a groove. If you are abstaining from food, your detox is over—or will be over very soon—and you should be feeling pretty good. Fasting seems to hit people differently, and I have not been able to fully understand why.

When I fast from food entirely, I have more energy, more focus, less pain, and rarely feel hungry. Overall, I feel better during a prolonged fast than at any other time of the year. I don't hear this from everyone, but I think they may not be staying committed to the fast. Because of this the cravings never stop, and the detox never takes place.

If you have fallen off the wagon, go ahead and get back up and start again. Dedicate this time to God and trust Him as you sacrifice. Remind yourself why you started the fast in the first place. If it was important enough to start, it is important enough to continue. Over time it will become easier, and the struggle will become less intense.

Action Steps:

1. Reaffirm Your Purpose: Take time to reflect on the reasons why you embarked on this fast in the first place. Remind yourself of the spiritual goals, intentions, and desires you set at the beginning of your fast. Consider the promises of Jeremiah 29:11 and meditate on God's plans for your welfare and future. Reconnecting with your purpose will reignite your motivation and commitment to continue the fast, even when faced with challenges or temptations.

2. Stay Resilient Through Challenges: Acknowledge that fasting can present various physical, mental, and emotional challenges, especially as you reach the midpoint of your fast. Be prepared to encounter moments of weakness, cravings, or doubts about continuing. However, instead of succumbing to these challenges, choose to persevere in your commitment to the fast. Lean on God's strength, and rely on His promises to sustain you through difficult times.

3. Focus on the Long-Term Benefits: Keep your eyes fixed on the long-term benefits and outcomes of your fast, rather than solely focusing on the temporary discomfort or sacrifices you may be experiencing. Remember that fasting is a spiritual discipline designed to draw you closer to God, enhance your prayer life, and align you with His will. Trust that as you remain faithful in your commitment to fasting and prayer, God will honor your obedience and bring about positive transformation in your life. Embrace the journey of fasting as an opportunity for growth, renewal, and deeper intimacy with God.

Journal

Day 4

FASTING FOR PEACE

Pastor Mike Harrell

Fuel Church of Lakeland, Florida

Anxiety and depression is higher now than at any time in recorded history. While there are many factors for the current trend, a bright spot in these studies reveals that people of faith have less depression and anxiety than others. Our hope is not anchored in our circumstances; it is anchored in the person of Jesus Christ. The fruit of a close relationship with Christ—among other things—is peace.

"Come to me, all who labor and are heavy laden,
and I will give you rest.
Take my yoke upon you, and learn from me,
for I am gentle and lowly in heart,
and you will find rest for your souls.
For my yoke is easy, and my burden is light."
Matthew 11:28-30 (ESV)

When bringing our burdens to Christ, we leave them at the foot of the cross with no need to pick them back up again. Worry is replaced with peace because we trust that He has good plans for us. We trust that He is sovereign over all things and nothing happens to us without first being filtered through His loving hands.

One of my favorite Scriptures is:

**"But now thus says the LORD, he who created you, O Jacob,
he who formed you, O Israel: 'Fear not, for I have redeemed you;
I have called you by name, you are mine.
When you pass through the waters, I will be with you;
and through the rivers, they shall not overwhelm you;
when you walk through fire you shall not be burned,
and the flame shall not consume you.'"
Isaiah 43:1-2 (ESV)**

With this passage I am reminded that I will have difficulties in life. I will walk through the fire, and I will walk through the river; but through it all the Lord will be with me. When we add fasting to our prayer life on a regular basis, we are intentional about growing closer in our relationship with the Lord. This will always result in an increase of the fruits of the Spirit and an increase of peace.

If you feel you are carrying a heavy burden, look to Jesus. It may be time to spend a few days of fasting while you pray about your situation. Once your fast is complete, patiently wait for God's timing and will to be accomplished; and rest in the peace of mind that He is already at work.

Action Steps:

1. Identify Areas of Anxiety and Burden: Take time to reflect on areas of your life where you may be experiencing anxiety, stress, or burdens. This could include personal challenges, relational conflicts, work pressures, or health concerns. Acknowledge these areas and recognize the impact they may have on your mental and emotional well-being. By identifying specific areas of anxiety or burden, you can bring them before the Lord in prayer and fasting, seeking His peace and intervention in those areas.

2. Commit to Intentional Fasting and Prayer: Make a deliberate decision to incorporate fasting into your prayer life as a means of seeking God's peace and provision. Choose a period of time, whether it's a day, several days, or a specific mealtime to dedicate yourself for the sole purpose of growing closer to God. Use Isaiah 43:1-2 as a foundation for your prayers, trusting in God's promise to be with you and to bring you through every trial and challenge.

3. Trust in God's Sovereignty and Timing: Throughout your fast, cultivate a spirit of trust and surrender, knowing that God is sovereign over all things and that He has good plans for your life. Release your anxieties and burdens into His capable hands, trusting that He will work all things together for your good and His glory. Resist the urge to pick up the burdens you've laid down in prayer, instead choosing to rest in God's peace and assurance. As you wait patiently for God's timing and will to be accomplished, continue to seek Him diligently through prayer and fasting, knowing that He is already at work in your situation.

Journal

Day 5

THE POWER OF PRAYER

Pastor Mark Epperson
Medulla Baptist Church of Lakeland, Florida

David, a man after God's own heart, is found crying out unto the Lord:

"I waited patiently for the Lord; and He inclined to me and heard my cry."
Psalm 40:1 (NASB)

Waiting patiently for the Lord to respond, David's cry was heard. God, our creator, who fixed the stars and galaxies, who perfectly designed this planet that it might sustain life, hears our cries. God not only hears, but He also answers:

"He brought me up out of the pit of destruction, out of the miry clay,
and He set my feet upon a rock making my footsteps firm.
He put a new song in my mouth, a song of praise to our God;
Many will see and fear And will trust in the Lord."
Psalm 40:2-3 (NASB)

God has a great track record of answering prayer: Abraham prayed; God provided a ram in the bush. Moses prayed; God parted the Red Sea. Gideon prayed; God gave him a sign. Hannah prayed;

God gave her a son. Elijah prayed; God sent down fire on Mount Carmel. Solomon prayed; God gave him wisdom. Hezekiah prayed; God added 15 years to his life. The disciples prayed; the Holy Spirit came down, and the church was born. Peter prayed; the lame man walked. Paul prayed; a European church was born at Philippi. Paul and Silas prayed; their Philippian jailhouse rocked, and the jailer was converted. John prayed; God gave him a Revelation for the future.

Jesus prayed! When Jesus prayed, Satan fled and multitudes were fed; the lame could walk and the dumb could talk; the blind could see and the demons would flee; the disciples He chose and Lazarus arose. When Jesus prayed, even the winds obeyed.

And late one night in agonizing prayer, Jesus cried out, "Father, if it be Thy will, let this cup pass from me; nevertheless, not My will but Thine be done." The Father answered, and Jesus willingly went to Calvary, taking upon Himself the sins of the world that our sins might be forgiven. Then three days later, Jesus rose from the dead, declaring victory over death, hell, and the grave!

Aren't you glad Jesus prayed? Aren't you glad the Father inclined to the Son's prayer and answered His cry? Oh, the power of prayer!

"What a friend we have in Jesus,
all our sins and griefs to bear;
What a privilege to carry
everything to God in prayer.
Oh, what peace we often forfeit,
oh, what needless pain we bear;
all because we do not carry
everything to God in prayer."
~ Joseph Medlicott Scriven

Action Step

Do you take the desires of your heart to God in prayer? God really does want to hear from us. Right now, like many of the men and women of the Scriptures, draw near to God through the power of prayer. Passionately make your requests known to Him. Pray in His will, and then remain alert with great sensitivity for how He answers and what He reveals.

Journal

Day 6

PRAYER BRINGS REVIVAL

Pastor Mark Epperson
Medulla Baptist Church of Lakeland, Florida

It is unclear at what point in his life David wrote the 40th Psalm. There are several possibilities. Perhaps David was in a dark place in his life, living in exile or living in sin. Nevertheless, as David cries out to the Lord,

"I waited patiently for the Lord; and He inclined to me and heard my cry."
Psalm 40:1 (NASB)

God hears and answers His cry, and a period of restoration and revival is experienced.

"He brought me up out of the pit of destruction, out of the miry clay,
and He set my feet upon a rock making my footsteps firm.
He put a new song in my mouth, a song of praise to our God;
Many will see and fear And will trust in the LORD."
Psalm 40:2-3 (NASB)

From David's life here, we have a picture of how prayer brings revival:

First, God provides *a fresh cleansing* as He brings David up from the pit of destruction, out of the miry clay. At times we might find ourselves in that pit, languishing away, wallowing in despair, defeat, or depravity. With no way to climb out on our own, we are destined for destruction if there is no restoration. However, just as the Gospel is the power of salvation for everyone who believes, prayer is the power of restoration through which God brings about a great work of revival through a fresh cleansing in His people.

Next, God provides for David *a clear awareness*. As we experience revival in our life, God sets our feet, giving us the proper direction, pointing us in the way we should go. He sets our feet upon the rock, the foundational truths of the perfect Word of God. Setting our feet upon that rock, God makes our footsteps firm, sanctifying our life, solidifying our position, and strengthening our mind.

Then, God gives David *a new song:* a song of praise. The next line is fascinating! Hearing is what is usually associated with "song." However, with this song, seeing is believing! The testimony of this new song is not just sung from the lips, but it is also made evident by what is seen in the life. Restoration and revival bring a new, living testimony that others will not just hear but will also see, fear, and . . . do you see it? They will trust in the Lord!

With genuine repentance through the power of prayer, God brings about restoration through a fresh cleansing, a clear awareness, and a new song. The spirit of the winds of revival blow, and a fresh fire begins to grow deep within the heart and life.

Action Step

Believer, do you need to be revived? You are saved, but spiritually you are on life support. Those who are without Christ don't really see anything different in your life than what is in their own. Right now, repent of the sin in your life that might be holding back God's blessings. As God cleanses you, get back into His Word. As you are living for Him, revived, the beauty of your "new song" will be evident to those around you . . . in particular, to those who are without Christ.

Journal

Day 7

FASTING IN FUTILITY

Pastor Mark Epperson
Medulla Baptist Church of Lakeland, Florida

"Now He also told this parable to some people who trusted in themselves that they were righteous, and viewed others with contempt:
'Two men went up into the temple to pray, one a Pharisee and the other a tax collector.
The Pharisee stood and *began* praying this in regard to himself:
"God, I thank You that I am not like other people:
swindlers, crooked, adulterers, or even like this tax collector.
I fast twice a week; I pay tithes of all that I get."
But the tax collector, standing some distance away,
was even unwilling to raise his eyes toward heaven,
but was beating his chest, saying, "God, be merciful to me, the sinner!"
'I tell you, this man went to his house justified rather than the other one;
for everyone who exalts himself will be humbled,
but the one who humbles himself will be exalted.'"
Luke 18:9-14 (NASB)

The observance of fasting was commanded by God in the Old Testament. While fasting is not commanded in the New Testament, it is certainly affirmed by Jesus and acknowledged as proper practice in other parts of the New Testament:

"But *the* days will come; and when the groom is taken away from them, then they will fast in those days."
Luke 5:35 (NASB)

Throughout Scripture fasting is almost always combined with prayer and offers believers a time to focus and hunger after God. Fasting is to be a private, personal act of devotion to God, an act that puts aside our pride, denies our desires, and searches the heart of God. Fasting is an action of personal humility and is not for public consumption:

"Now whenever you fast, do not make a gloomy face as the hypocrites *do*,
for they distort their faces
so that they will be noticed by people when they are fasting.
Truly I say to you, they have their reward in full.
But as for you, when you fast, anoint your head and wash your face,
so that your fasting will not be noticed by people
but by your Father who is in secret;
and your Father who sees *what is done* in secret will reward you."
Matthew 6:16-18 (NASB)

In Jesus' parable in Luke 18, our dear Pharisee, while praying, was going about it all wrong. Before what was likely a large audience at the Temple in Jerusalem, he stood and pompously declared (among other things) that along with paying tithes of all his increase, he fasts twice a week. Boastful and full of pride, this Pharisee wasn't praying to God but to himself and, as Jesus stated, with a clear objective of making it a public display for those listening at the Temple. With this boastful claim, even if true, his fasting was useless and spiritually meaningless. As arrogant and open with his claim as he was, this Pharisee was absolutely fasting in futility.

When we go into times of fasting, we do so to draw nearer to God, to know more of who He is, to desire a cleansing and purifying of our soul, and to draw on His wisdom and direction for our life. We do this without any attempt or desire for the recognition of man. If done in this way, fasting will produce fruitfulness. Otherwise, we will also be fasting in futility.

Is there a problem or problems you are facing that seem too much to bear? Prayer combined with fasting may be the focus you need. Many of the people in Scripture and throughout church history who practiced fasting were mightily used by God. At the very least, to fast in a Scriptural way as Jesus taught will certainly be exalted by God. Fast in humility rather than futility.

Action Step

When was the last time you personally fasted? Often there are times we need to draw nearer to the Lord, which is the benefit of fasting. Right now, ask the Lord for guidance in setting aside some time to fast. Be willing to decline a physical need for a while in order to fulfill a spiritual need. Humbly and privately get before the Lord; and with His Word receive His nourishment for spiritual wisdom, healing, and guidance.

Journal

Day 8

FASTING FOR LEADERSHIP

Pastor Mark Epperson
Medulla Baptist Church of Lakeland, Florida

Serving as a model for every Christian and every church when it comes to selecting leadership is the practice of prayer and fasting as accomplished by the first-century church. In each of these passages below, the people of the church were found praying and fasting.

Here, the Holy Spirit provided direction for the church in setting apart those for the work of spiritual leadership:

**"Now there were prophets and teachers at Antioch,
in the church that was *there*:
Barnabas, Simeon who was called Niger, Lucius of Cyrene,
Manaen who had been brought up
with Herod the tetrarch, and Saul.
While they were serving the Lord and fasting,
the Holy Spirit said, 'Set Barnabas and Saul apart for Me for the
work to which I have called them.'
Then, when they had fasted, prayed, and laid their hands
on them, they sent them away."
Acts 13:1-3 (NASB)**

Then, in Acts 14 the Lord gave direction to Paul and Barnabas as to whom the appointed leaders were to be in each church:

"And after they had preached the gospel to that city and had made a good number of disciples, they returned to Lystra, to Iconium, and to Antioch, strengthening the souls of the disciples, encouraging them to continue in the faith, and *saying*, '*It is* through many tribulations *that* we must enter the kingdom of God.' When they had appointed elders for them in every church, having prayed with fasting, they entrusted them to the Lord in whom they had believed."
Acts 14:21-23 (NASB)

Years earlier, before He chose His disciples, Jesus fasted and prayed. Sadly, this would be a novel idea for most churches today.

While I was serving on a church staff, our pastor resigned to take an Associational Director of Missions position. The first act of our Pastor Search Committee was to appoint a chairman. Jokingly, but true to form of many committees, they chose the one member who was not able to make the first meeting! That member, by the way, did not regularly attend our worship services, either.

As our committee went about its work, they quickly focused on one individual. It was not long before they decided to bring him "in view of a call" (the Baptist way of having him preach before the congregation and then voted on). With what I thought was a hastily-made decision, I tried to get information from committee members regarding the prospective pastor. I didn't learn anything about his doctrine, his beliefs, or his administrative skills; but I was told by one of the members, "He sure is nice-looking!"

Oh, brothers and sisters! When calling leadership to the church or selecting leaders within the ministry of the church, left up to our own desires, devices, and decisions, we often fail. The first-century church got it right! As we seek leadership in calling a pastor or staff member or selecting deacons, elders, or teachers from within, fasting and praying will prompt the movement of the Holy Spirit, who will provide direction for the choosing of that leadership.

Action Step

You have probably prayed for the leadership of your church many times, but have you ever prayed and fasted for those leaders? Set aside a time this week—as well as on a regular basis—for fasting for those who hold leadership positions in your church, that all of you as a church family will follow the prompting of the Holy Spirit as He directs for any and all decisions that are to be made.

Journal

Day 9

GOD'S THRONE ROOM

Dr. Lanelle Pickett, Sr.
Good Hope Missionary Baptist Church of Bartow, Florida

"Be anxious for nothing, but in everything by prayer and supplication, with thanksgiving, let your requests be made known to God; and the peace of God which surpasses all understanding, w ill guard your hearts and minds through Christ Jesus."
Philippians 4:6-7 (NKJV)

One of the many blessings afforded to Christ followers is prayer. We can enter into His presence, His "Throne Room," for a talk with our loving, gracious, kind, merciful, forgiving God at any time, from any place, and for any reason. Imagine, while there in the presence of your Loving Heavenly Father, you can share in complete confidence any topic you desire. That's right! Whatever is near and dear to your heart, express it. Do you have concerns about your marriage, family, health, neighbors, friends, career, church, spiritual growth? No problem, as a believer in Jesus Christ, God will hear and answer your prayers. With that in mind, go into His presence (Throne Room) often, and enjoy sweet fellowship with your Heavenly Father.

Action Step

Take a moment to pause and reflect on your prayer life. Are you spending quality time alone with God in prayer? Each day, imagine your loving, Heavenly Father awaiting your presence in His Throne Room. Enter in, and enjoy the wondrous privilege of His presence in prayer.

Journal

Day 10

THE GOD WHO ANSWERS PRAYER

Dr. Lanelle Pickett, Sr.
Good Hope Missionary Baptist Church of Bartow, Florida

**"Then Jehoshaphat stood in the assembly of Judah and Jerusalem,
in the house of the LORD, before the new court, and said:
'O LORD God of our fathers, *are* You not God in heaven,
and do You *not* rule over all the kingdoms of the nations,
and in Your hand *is there not* power and might,
so that no one is able to withstand You?'"
2 Chronicles 20:5-6 (NKJV)**

King Jehoshaphat of Judah received word that he and the people were about to be attacked by a great multitude. He knew that the small military force of Judah was not capable of standing against the combined super force of Ammon, Moab, and Mt. Seir. So, with disaster lurking on the horizon, all the people of Judah gathered to ask for help from the Lord. King Jehoshaphat led the prayer meeting and concluded with the words:

**"For we have no power against this great multitude
that is coming against us;
nor do we know what to do, but our eyes *are* upon You."
2 Chronicles 20:12b (NKJV)**

With these words of prayer, Jehoshaphat and the people trusted God; and God delivered them.

The reality is people, pressures, and problems will come that exceed your ability to handle them. Issues will unfold, circumstances will arise, and situations will develop that threaten to bring you down. When such times occur, don't wait; swiftly take the matter(s) to God in prayer. Your Heavenly Father (The God Who Answers Prayer) has the power to do and will do whatever needs to be done to take care of you. And should you have any doubt, fear, or hesitation, let your mind go back to Calvary; and see in action the God who answers prayer on your behalf.

Action Step

Write down your most challenging situation right now. Commit that to God in prayer. He is willing and able to help you overcome any obstacle you are facing.

Journal

Day 11

THE MYSTERY OF PRAYER

Dr. Lanelle Pickett, Sr.
Good Hope Missionary Baptist Church of Bartow, Florida

"Return and tell Hezekiah the leader of My people,
'Thus says the Lord, the God of David your father:
"I have heard your prayer, I have seen your tears;
surely I will heal you.
On the third day you shall go up to the house of the Lord.
And I will add to your days fifteen years.
I will deliver you and this city from the hand of the king of Assyria; and I will defend this city for My own sake,
and for the sake of My servant David."'
2 Kings 20:5-6 (NKJV)

In today's Scripture lesson, Hezekiah, King of Judah, was sick and near death. Hezekiah was a good king whose life and leadership were characterized by prayer and faithfulness to God. While on his sick bed, the prophet, Isaiah, delivered a message to Hezekiah from God:

"Thus says the Lord: 'Set your house in order, for you shall die, and not live.'"
2 Kings 20:1 (NKJV)

Hezekiah turned his face to the wall and prayed, asking God to remember how he had walked before Him in truth, how his heart was loyal, and how he had done good in the sight of God. Then Hezekiah wept bitterly.

Shortly thereafter, God sent Isaiah back to the king with another message:

"I have heard your prayer, I have seen your tears; surely I will heal you.
On the third day you shall go up to the house of the Lord.
And I will add to your days fifteen years.
I will deliver you and this city from the hand of the king of Assyria."
2 Kings 20:5-6 (NKJV)

Therein lies the mystery of prayer. One season the king is on his death bed; the next season he is a picture of health. Here's the takeaway: as a believer in Jesus Christ, you will not always know how God will work things out on your behalf. Nevertheless, you can always pray and trust God to work things out for His glory and your good . . . even when His work is a mystery.

Henry Blackaby, author of *Experiencing God*, said, "God is always at work around you." All the details of His work may not be known, yet the *benefits* of His work will be evident.

Action Step

Have fun exploring God's mysteries. A great way to do this is to keep a prayer journal. Write down what you are praying for, update each entry periodically, and then be specific about how God answers each prayer. As you review your growing number of completed prayer entries, you will better understand how God responds to your requests. Answered prayer will become less of a mystery, and your confidence in asking things from God will grow!

Journal

Day 12

EYE-OPENING PRAYER

Dr. Lanelle Pickett, Sr.
Good Hope Missionary Baptist Church of Bartow, Florida

"And Elisha prayed, and said,
'Lord, I pray, open his eyes that he may see.'
Then the Lord opened the eyes of the young man, and he saw. And behold, the mountain *was* full of horses and chariots of fire all around Elisha."
2 Kings 6:17 (NKJV)

The background of this text reveals Syria is at war with Israel; but each time the Syrian king planned an attack against Israel, his plan failed. Believing that one among his servants was a traitor, he confronted them. To his dismay he found that Elisha, the prophet, was revealing his secrets to the king of Israel. Frustrated and furious, the Syrian king surrounded the city of Dothan to capture Elisha.

When Elisha's servant arose early and went outside, there was the enemy's army surrounding the city with horses and chariots. Now, in panic mode Elisha's servant asked, "What shall we do?" Instead of giving his servant a pep talk or 10 steps to overcoming panic, Elisha prayed, "Lord, I pray, open his eyes that he may see." Then the Lord opened the servant's eyes to see the mountain full of horses and chariots of fire all around Elisha.

The truth is some days you will be surrounded by enemies such as fear, foolishness, and frustrations. Some days the enemies will be doubt, depression, and deception. Some days the enemies will be intimidation, insecurity, and inadequacy. No matter what constitutes your fear, quickly pray the "Eye-Opening Prayer." Ask God to open your eyes so you can see every high mountain, every low valley, every tumultuous storm, and every raging sea from His perspective. With his spiritual eyes wide open, Elisha's servant saw the presence, peace, and protection of God . . . and so will you.

Action Step

Make a list of fears you are facing right now. Surrender your areas of fear to God. Ask Him to open your eyes that you may see His mighty power working in, through, and around you.

Journal

Day 13

PRAYING FOR YOUR CHURCH

Dr. Richard Williamson
Central Florida Baptist Association

**"In addition, brothers and sisters, pray for us
that the word of the Lord may spread rapidly
and be honored, just as it was with you,
and that we may be delivered from wicked and evil people,
for not all have faith.
But the Lord is faithful; he will strengthen you
and guard you from the evil one.
We have confidence in the Lord about you,
that you are doing and will continue to do what we command.
May the Lord direct your hearts to God's love and Christ's endurance."
2 Thessalonians 3:1-5 (CSB)**

Hearing others pray is how we often first learn to pray. This is why I think it is so important to read the prayers of Scripture. In them, we can see how Jesus and the early church leaders prayed. They can help us see what we ought to be praying for.

In this passage we see three things:

- Paul's personal prayer request
- Why we can be confident in prayer
- What Paul prayed for regarding the church at Thessalonica

First, Paul asks the Thessalonians to pray for him. He wants the Word of God to spread quickly; he wants people to obey the Word; and he wants to avoid evil people. These are things we can pray for today.

In verses three and four Paul shares why he is confident about his prayers. He reminds his readers that the Lord is faithful and that we can have confidence in Him. We need to remember these same things as we pray for our church.

Finally, Paul asks God to direct the Thessalonians' hearts to two things: God's love and Christ's endurance. We need these same two items to guide us. We need to be church members who exhibit both love and endurance that we have learned from God.

Action Steps

As you pray . . .

1. *Pray for the ministry of your church.*
2. *Pray that the Word will spread quickly through its ministries and that those who hear the Word will obey it.*
3. *Pray that your church would be spared from evil people.*
4. *Pray with confidence.*
5. *Know that God is faithful and trustworthy.*
6. *Pray for the people of your church that they would walk in love and endurance.*

Journal

Day 14

PRAYING FOR MORE OF GOD

Dr. Richard Williamson
Central Florida Baptist Association

"'Now if I have indeed found favor with you,
please teach me your ways, and I will know you,
so that I may find favor with you.
Now consider that this nation is your people.'
And he replied, 'My presence will go with you, and I will give you rest.'
'If your presence does not go,' Moses responded to him,
'don't make us go up from here.
How will it be known that I and your people have found favor
with you unless you go with us?
I and your people will be distinguished by this
from all the other people on the face of the earth.'
The Lord answered Moses, 'I will do this very thing you have asked,
for you have found favor with me, and I know you by name.'
Then Moses said, 'Please, let me see your glory.'"
Exodus 33:13-18 (CSB)

This is one of my favorite prayers in the Bible. It is a conversation between God and Moses. This simple conversation is a reminder for us that our prayers are simply a conversation between us and God, as well.

In this prayer Moses made two big requests and responded to a declaration of God. Each of these is a reminder of how dependent we are on God.

First, Moses has a request for God: *teach me your ways*. Moses does not want to stay who he is, he wants to be more like God. Scripture tells us that His ways are higher than our ways:

> **"For as heaven is higher than earth,**
> **so my ways are higher than your ways,**
> **and my thoughts than your thoughts."**
> **Isaiah 55:9 (CSB)**

In response to God's saying that His presence would go with Moses and the people, Moses asked that *they not be made to go anywhere alone*. As Christians we have been given the Spirit of God. I just wonder how mindful we are of the presence of God. How much do we desire to live all our lives in His presence?

Finally, Moses asked to *see the glory of God*. Moses had seen a partial display of God's glory in the burning bush (Exodus 3), and it left him wanting more. We have seen a partial display of God's glory in our lives through His Word and His work in us. Here is the big question: are we hungry for more?

Action Steps

As you pray . . .

1. *Are you asking God to teach you His ways or do you think you know enough already?*
2. *Are you mindful and thankful of the presence of God in your daily life?*
3. *Do you want more of Him?*

Journal

Day 15

PRAYING FOR WHAT REALLY MATTERS

Dr. Richard Williamson
Central Florida Baptist Association

"We always thank God, the Father of our Lord Jesus Christ, when we pray for you, for we have heard of your faith in Christ Jesus and of the love you have for all the saints because of the hope reserved for you in heaven. You have already heard about this hope in the word of truth, the gospel that has come to you. It is bearing fruit and growing all over the world, just as it has among you since the day you heard it and came to truly appreciate God's grace. You learned this from Epaphras, our dearly loved fellow servant. He is a faithful minister of Christ on your behalf, and he has told us about your love in the Spirit."
Colossians 1:3-8 (CSB)

In this passage of Scripture, Paul gives thanks for the believers at Colossae. The things that he gives thanks for are important enough that he thanked God for them and then wrote an encouraging note about them to the Colossians. These items are the start of a good list of things to regularly thank God for.

First, Paul gave thanks for their *faith in Jesus*. We should regularly give thanks for the fact that we have come into a right relationship with God through faith. We should also pray for others to come to know Him.

Next, he is thankful for their *love for the saints*. The term, "saints," refers to other believers. We ought to pray that our love for other believers will grow more and more!

Then, he is thankful that the Gospel is bearing fruit around the world. This is something that we should both give thanks for and regularly pray for. We can pray for those missionaries who are taking the Gospel around the world and that God would bless their efforts.

Finally, Paul mentions Epaphras who was a faithful minister and had taught the Colossians the Gospel. This reminds us to both give thanks for and pray for the faithful ministers in our lives.

Action Step

Make a list before you pray . . .

1. *Who do you know who needs to come to faith in Jesus?*
2. *Which believer do you need to love more today?*
3. *What missionary do you know who is taking the Gospel around the world?*
4. *Who is a spiritual mentor to you?*

Journal

Day 16

WHY WE FAST

Dr. Richard Williamson
Central Florida Baptist Association

**"Then John's disciples came to him, saying,
'Why do we and the Pharisees fast often, but your disciples do not fast?'
Jesus said to them, 'Can the wedding guests be sad
while the groom is with them?
The time will come when the groom will be taken away from them,
and then they will fast.'"
Matthew 9:14-15 (CSB)**

In these verses Jesus is asked why His disciples did not fast. Jesus basically responds that it was because He was there with them. He goes on to say that there was a time coming when He would be taken away, and then His disciples would fast.

Today followers of Christ live in the time where Jesus has gone away. He has promised to return, but for now He has gone away.

**"Don't let your heart be troubled. Believe in God; believe also in me.
In my Father's house are many rooms.
If it were not so, would I have told you
that I am going to prepare a place for you?**

If I go away and prepare a place for you,
I will come again and take you to myself,
so that where I am you may be also."
John 14:1-3 (CSB)

As His disciples, we should be longing for His return.

"There is reserved for me the crown of righteousness,
which the Lord, the righteous Judge, will give me on that day,
and not only to me, but to all those who have loved his appearing."
2 Timothy 4:8 (CSB)

The crown of righteousness is reserved for those who love or long for (depending on your Bible version) His return. Either way, for the believer there ought to be real joy when we think of Christ's return and a longing for it to happen soon.

This leads us to why we fast. We fast because we long for the Lord to return and look forward to being with Him. We live in a world where things are not as they ought to be. We inhabit a dark and fallen world. However, one day Jesus will return and take us home.

Life is busy, and it has a way of taking our minds off the things that really matter. Fasting helps refocus our minds on the centrality of Jesus in our lives and our longing to be with him.

Action Step

Ask yourself . . .

1. *What can you give up so that you can focus on what really matters?*
2. *How much do you long for the return of Jesus?*

Journal

Day 17

HUNGER AND THIRST

Pastor Jason Seger

Revive Church of Lakeland, Florida

"Blessed are the poor in spirit, for theirs is the kingdom of heaven.
Blessed are those who mourn, for they will be comforted.
Blessed are the meek, for they will inherit the earth.
Blessed are those who hunger and thirst for righteousness,
for they will be filled.
Blessed are the merciful, for they will be shown mercy.
Blessed are the pure in heart, for they will see God.
Blessed are the peacemakers, for they will be called children of God.
Blessed are those who are persecuted because of righteousness,
for theirs is the kingdom of heaven."
Matthew 5:3-10 (NIV)

This introduction to the Sermon on the Mount sets the stage for the radically different kind of life Jesus wants us to live. How is it possible to live that kind of life, though? It sounds almost impossible. Our hearts don't naturally long to be meek, merciful, poor in spirit, or peacemakers. How do we make that shift?

"Blessed are those who hunger and thirst for righteousness . . ."
Matthew 5:6 (NIV)

We have to change our deepest cravings. In Jesus' words we need to learn to "hunger and thirst for righteousness," to hunger and thirst for Him. The deprivation of fasting helps with that.

I just read an article on the Carnivore Diet. It's a diet where one only eats meat. After two days the author was ferociously craving all the things he had been denying himself. He thought he had what he *wanted*; but in reality, he was missing something he *needed.*

When we fast, the first response is to crave food. The second response is to crave the sustaining power of God. Stripping away the things we think we want reveals what we truly *need.* As we linger in that place of dependance on God, He teaches us to hunger and thirst for more of Him; and that is the place where the heart Jesus described in Matthew 5 is formed.

Action Step

Block out some time for prayer and fasting this week. Read Matthew 5-7. Ask God to show you where you're out of line with it, and ask for a hunger for Him that shapes your heart into His image. He promised that hungering and thirsting for righteousness would lead to being filled.

Journal

Day 18

FIRST STEP OF FAITH

Pastor Jason Seger
Revive Church of Lakeland, Florida

I don't know about you but when things go wrong, I tend to want to jump into "fix-it" mode. How can I fix this problem? How can I make this better?

That's not the example Nehemiah set, though. When he heard the walls of Jerusalem were still broken down and that God's people were in distress, Nehemiah stopped and prayed . . . not just a prayer, but he prayed and fasted for days. Instead of trying to fix the problem on his own, he went to God with trust and expectation.

Fasting was Nehemiah's first step of faith. Nehemiah trusted God to sustain him. His job as cupbearer was important and required him to perform well physically and mentally. Nehemiah's first step of faith was to trust that to God while he sought God's help.

"Then I said: 'LORD, the God of heaven, the great and awesome God,
who keeps his covenant of love with those who love him
and keep his commandments,
let your ear be attentive and your eyes open to hear the prayer
your servant is praying before you day and night for your servants,
the people of Israel.

I confess the sins we Israelites, including myself and my father's family,
have committed against you.
We have acted very wickedly toward you.
We have not obeyed the commands, decrees and laws
you gave your servant Moses.
Remember the instruction you gave your servant Moses, saying,
"If you are unfaithful, I will scatter you among the nations,
but if you return to me and obey my commands,
then even if your exiled people are at the farthest horizon,
I will gather them from there and bring them to the place
I have chosen as a dwelling for my Name."
They are your servants and your people,
whom you redeemed by your great strength and your mighty hand.
Lord, let your ear be attentive to the prayer of this your servant
and to the prayer of your servants who delight in revering your name.
Give your servant success today by granting him favor
in the presence of this man.'"
Nehemiah 1:5-10 (NIV)

His prayer in chapter 1 shows a heart that has been formed through deep faith and reliance on God. Nehemiah confesses his nation's sin, celebrates God's faithfulness and strength, and asks for God to move on their behalf.

God's response is quick and overwhelming. That's not always the case, but the faith we are trying to develop is one that trusts God no matter the answer. In Nehemiah's case God gives him favor with the king, and all that Nehemiah needed to help his people was provided.

This isn't a one-time occurrence, though. We see Nehemiah face every obstacle with faith and prayer throughout the rest of the book as he seeks to help his people rebuild.

Action Step

What obstacle are you facing right now? Instead of immediately jumping in with both feet to try to fix it yourself, take some time to pray and fast. Trust God to sustain you and to provide what you need. Let this process develop in your heart so that your faith and reliance on God grows. Your first step of faith may drastically change the course of your life.

Journal

Day 19

LOOK WHAT I FOUND

Pastor Jason Seger
Revive Church of Lakeland, Florida

Have you ever found something you didn't know you lost? You know, you open a box that got shoved under your bed, find an envelope in a drawer, go up to the attic for the first time in months, and there it is. You may not have realized it was missing, but you're glad you found it.

That's what happened to Josiah. In 2 Kings 22 Josiah sends some men to the temple to give the high priest a message about a building project. Hilkiah, the priest, sends the men back with a different message: he found a book . . . not just any book; he found the Word of God. It had been lost for so long that his generation didn't even know it was missing.

Second Kings 23 outlines Josiah's reforms in response to what he found in the pages of God's Word. Here's what we learn from Josiah about revival: it starts with our response to God's Word. As he read God's Word for the first time, Josiah was confronted by the reality that he and his people had sinned greatly against God. He immediately repented by removing the idols and stopping the worship of false gods. Repentance, or turning from sin to God, is a necessary part of revival and is the evidence of a genuine response to God.

**"If we confess our sins, he is faithful and just
and will forgive us our sins and purify us from all unrighteousness."
1 John 1:9 (NIV)**

**"The king stood by the pillar and renewed the covenant
in the presence of the LORD—to follow the LORD and keep his commands,
statutes and decrees with all his heart and all his soul . . .."
2 Kings 23:3 (NIV)**

If you read the rest of chapter 23, you'll get the sense that turning back to God is difficult and costly . . . but also worth it. Like Josiah, we can sometimes find ourselves way off course with a lot to do to get back, but the beauty of God's grace is that He sees our heart as well as our actions. In Chapter 22 a prophet told Josiah that God heard his prayer, saw his repentance, and would spare his life.

**"Neither before nor after Josiah was there a king like him
who turned to the Lord as he did—
with all his heart and with all his soul and with all his strength,
in accordance with all the Law of Moses."
2 Kings 23:25 (NIV)**

Action Step

Have you wandered from God? Start the process of coming back by pursuing Him through reading His Word and connecting to a local church. Then step-by-step turn away from the sinful thoughts, actions, and attitudes He shows you and turn toward Him.

Journal

Day 20

ONE CHANGED HEART

Pastor Jason Seger
Revive Church of Lakeland, Florida

"It only takes a spark to get a fire going. . . ." That's the first line of a praise song from the late 60s called "Pass it On." Kurt Kaiser wrote the song to capture the hearts of teens and to encourage them to pass on the love of God. The woman Jesus encountered in John 4 lived a long time before that song was written, but she became the spark that ignited a blaze in her hometown.

There is so much I love about John 4: Jesus sought out the Samaritan woman in spite of cultural boundaries; she worked through her own baggage to receive His love; and she becomes an unlikely evangelist with no training who kind of jumbles up the message and yet turns the hearts of a village to Jesus.

"Many of the Samaritans from that town believed in him because of the woman's testimony, 'He told me everything I ever did.'"
John 4:39 (NIV)

Do you see yourself in this passage? It has my name written all over it. I was lost and He found me; I struggled to wrap my head around the goodness of God and what He offers me; and I am positioned to be used by Him to tell His story to my village . . . and that's also true of you.

Action Step

You can be the one changed heart that God uses to draw others. Will you commit to that? I invite you to pray that God will continue to change your heart by His love and that He will give you opportunities to tell everyone you know about the Man who told you everything about yourself, including your acceptance of the hope of eternal life that's only found in Him.

Journal

Day 21

PLEADING WITH GOD

Dr. Matt McCraw
First Baptist Church of Bartow, Florida

**"So we fasted and pleaded with our God about this,
and he was receptive to our prayer."
Ezra 8:23 (CSB)**

Have you ever been so desperate for something that you pleaded for it? My kids plead quite often. "Dad, can we *please* go in the pool today?" "Dad, may I *please* have my phone back? I promise I'll be good." "Dad, may I *please* be excused from eating all of my food?" Most of us know what it means to plead.

Have you ever pleaded with God? Perhaps you pleaded for Him to help you pass a test when you were in school. Maybe you pleaded with Him that the law enforcement official who just pulled you over would decide to let you off with a warning. Maybe it was something more serious. Some of us have pleaded with God for our churches to grow closer to Him. Some of us have pleaded that a family member would be changed by the Gospel of Jesus.

**"I proclaimed a fast by the Ahava River,
so that we might humble ourselves before our God
and ask him for a safe journey for us,**

our dependents, and all our possessions.
I did this because I was ashamed to ask the king for infantry and cavalry to protect us from enemies during the journey, since we had told him, 'The hand of our God is gracious to all who seek him,
but his fierce anger is against all who abandon him.'
So we fasted and pleaded with our God about this,
and he was receptive to our prayer."
Ezra 8:21-23 (CSB)

To *plead* means to appeal or ask intently. In Ezra 8:21-23 we see an intent appeal from Ezra on behalf of the Jewish people to the God of all things. Ezra and the people were dependent upon God for their return from exile into Jerusalem. The journey and the rebuilding of Jerusalem would not be easy. So, they sought the Lord through fasting and prayer.

Fasting is particularly beneficial when someone wants to plead before the Lord. You see, fasting provides a continual reminder that we are hungry. It's a natural reaction to not eating. That natural reaction serves to prompt us to do a *super*natural act. Fasting reminds us to plead to God for His blessing.

Ezra and the people pleaded to God through fasting and prayer. So, also, God's people today must plead with Him for His guidance and blessing. Fasting will help you remember how much you need God and provides an avenue for you to plead to Him.

Action Step

Think about when you last pleaded before God. For what did you plead? How do you feel God answered? Have you considered fasting as a means of pleading to God?

Journal

Day 22

PRAYER 101

Dr. Matt McCraw

First Baptist Church of Bartow, Florida

"But when you pray, go into your private room, shut your door,
and pray to your Father who is in secret.
And your Father who sees in secret will reward you."
Matthew 6:6 (CSB)

These days we can find a lot of information about how to do things simply by visiting the Internet. We can watch "how to" videos, read manuals, and even take online classes. It would be nice if we had a "how to" manual on how to live out certain aspects of our Christian faith. The reality is, we do. The Bible serves as our guide for understanding who God is, who we are, and how we are to live the life that God wants for us.

A wonderful passage that serves as a "how to" for our prayer life is Matthew 6:5-13:

"Whenever you pray, you must not be like the hypocrites,
because they love to pray standing in the synagogues
and on the street corners to be seen by people.
Truly I tell you, they have their reward.

But when you pray, go into your private room, shut your door,
and pray to your Father who is in secret.
And your Father who sees in secret will reward you.
When you pray, don't babble like the Gentiles,
since they imagine they'll be heard for their many words.
Don't be like them,
because your Father knows the things you need before you ask him.
Therefore, you should pray like this:
Our Father in heaven, your name be honored as holy.
Your kingdom come. Your will be done on earth as it is in heaven.
Give us today our daily bread.
And forgive us our debts, as we also have forgiven our debtors.
And do not bring us into temptation, but deliver us from the evil one."
Matthew 6:5-13 (CSB)

These verses contain instructions directly from Jesus for how we should pray. Notice how Jesus begins. He says, "Whenever you pray." Jesus leaves no room for us not to pray. The people of God should be a praying people. So, when you pray, follow these tips from Jesus:

First, don't pray to show off in front of others (verse 5). Prayer is about communicating with God, not with others. So, don't seek to impress others; rather seek to be intimate with God (verse 6).

Second, don't attempt to impress others with your fancy language (verse 7). We can't impress God, and it's not important what others think about our prayers. So, pray simply and genuinely to God. He knows us, and He wants to hear from us (verse 8). Jesus even helps us by providing a model prayer for us. This model prayer further helps us understand how to pray.

A *third* element of our prayer lives should include acknowledging God's greatness and our desire to see Him carry out his work (verses 9-10).

Finally, we should ask God for provision for both our physical needs and our spiritual needs (verses 11-13).

So, how should we pray? Well, it's not complicated. It's not about being impressive. If you want to be someone who prays well, simply follow the instructions of Jesus.

Action Step

Write down the four elements of prayer and reflect upon the pattern as you pray this next week. See how God shapes your prayer life.

Journal

Day 23

THE GIFTS OF A GOOD FATHER

Dr. Matt McCraw
First Baptist Church of Bartow, Florida

Have you ever thought about what makes a good gift? Perhaps a good gift is something that you really *want*, or maybe it's something that you really *need*. Probably the best gift is something that you both *need and want*.

Think for a moment about the person who gives you the best gifts. It's usually someone who not only knows you well, but they really understand you. So, the best gifts are both what we want and need, given to us by someone who really understands us.

Do you know anyone who would perfectly be able to meet all these criteria? Of course you do, right? God the Father perfectly knows what we want; He perfectly knows what we need; and He perfectly understands us better than anyone. Jesus makes it clear for us in Matthew 7:7-11 that we can confidently go to God with our requests. We can pray to Him and have confidence that He will grant our requests in a way that is wise, loving, and helpful.

"Ask, and it will be given to you. Seek, and you will find.
Knock, and the door will be opened to you.
For everyone who asks receives, and the one who seeks finds,
and to the one who knocks, the door will be opened.

Who among you, if his son asks him for bread, will give him a stone?
Or if he asks for a fish, will give him a snake?
If you then, who are evil, know how to give good gifts to your children,
how much more will your Father in heaven
give good things to those who ask him."
Matthew 7:7-11 (CSB)

Jesus provides an example of a child asking their parent for something. Children don't have trouble asking for something, do they? Neither should we have trouble asking our Heavenly Father for something. At the same time, a parent will not give something to their child that is harmful to them. Likewise, God will not give us (His children) anything that is harmful to us.

"... how much more will your Father in heaven give good things
to those who ask him."
Matthew 7:11 (CSB)

So, when you request something in prayer, pray with confidence. Have confidence that you can give God your requests and have confidence that you can trust Him to provide that which is good for you. He is a good Father.

Action Step

Write down a list of requests you have for God. Underneath them, write down your motivation for asking for those requests. What does the Bible say in this passage (and elsewhere) about your requests?

Journal

Day 24

NEVER A MOMENT AWAY FROM PRAYER

Dr. Matt McCraw
First Baptist Church of Bartow, Florida

"Pray constantly."
1 Thessalonians 5:17 (CSB)

First Thessalonians 5:17 is a verse that many Christians know. It's translated in several different ways: "Pray constantly." (CSB) "Pray without ceasing." (KJV) "Never stop praying." (NLT) No matter the translation, the point remains the same: we are to always be in a continual spirit of prayer.

The meaning of the verse is simple. However, how we live out that verse may be a bit more confusing. How are we to pray constantly?

Let's first establish what this verse doesn't mean. It does not mean that we are to babble throughout the day for 24 hours. In fact, Scripture tells us elsewhere not to babble on.

"When you pray, don't babble like the Gentiles,
since they imagine they'll be heard for their many words."
Matthew 6:7 (CSB)

Also, it doesn't mean that we are to isolate ourselves, free from conservation with other people.

What the Apostle Paul probably means when he tells us to pray constantly is to be in a constant spirit of prayer. Another way to think about it is to think of being just a moment away from praying at every moment of the day. In short, we are to pray a lot. Prayer should always be on our minds and on our lips.

So, as you are driving in your car, think of how you can pray for requests that the Lord lays on your mind. When you face a challenge or heartache throughout the day, pray to God for comfort or strength. When you witness the beauty of a sunrise or a cool evening sky, praise God for his sovereign hand over creation. When you find your keys that you lost last night, thank God for that little blessing. Pray constantly. As you do, you will maintain the spiritual connection and loving intimacy with your Heavenly Father.

Action Step

Set a reminder on your phone or watch to pray a short prayer once every so often throughout the day. Seek to increase the frequency later. See how God shapes your prayer life.

Journal

Day 25

FASTING FOR THE RIGHT REASON

Pastor Matt Ellis

First Baptist Church of Polk City, Florida

Religious hypocrites often do the right things but for the wrong reasons. They may give to people in poverty, pray, or fast (which are good things!); but their ultimate desire is for others to see them and applaud. Their actions are good, but their motives are bad. And that's what we hear Jesus condemning in Matthew 6:1-6:

"Be careful not to practice your righteousness
in front of others to be seen by them.
Otherwise, you have no reward with your Father in heaven.
So whenever you give to the poor, don't sound a trumpet before you,
as the hypocrites do in the synagogues and on the streets,
to be applauded by people.
Truly I tell you, they have their reward.
But when you give to the poor,
don't let your left hand know what your right hand is doing,
so that your giving may be in secret.
And your Father who sees in secret will reward you.
Whenever you pray, you must not be like the hypocrites,
because they love to pray standing in the synagogues
and on the street corners to be seen by people.
Truly I tell you, they have their reward.

But when you pray, go into your private room, shut your door,
and pray to your Father who is in secret.
And your Father who sees in secret will reward you.
Matthew 6:1-6 (CSB)

After talking about how His followers needed to give to those in poverty and pray with pure motives, Jesus addressed the spiritual discipline of fasting in Matthew 6:16-18:

"Whenever you fast, don't be gloomy like the hypocrites.
For they disfigure their faces so that their fasting is obvious to people.
Truly I tell you, they have their reward.
But when you fast, put oil on your head and wash your face,
so that your fasting isn't obvious to others
but to your Father who is in secret.
And your Father who sees in secret will reward you."
Matthew 6:16-18 (CSB)

Jesus didn't present fasting as an option but as something He assumed His followers would do. He said, "*When* you fast . . .." There should be times when we give up food to refocus our spiritual energies and regain control of our indulgent propensities.

However, in this text Jesus demonstrated His knowledge of the human heart. We want others to think well of us. Like the religious hypocrites of Jesus' day, we may try to find happiness by impressing others with our spiritual activity. And when we do that, we destroy a good thing with a bad motive.

The reason Jesus gives for keeping our fasting to ourselves is interesting. He focuses on rewards. He essentially says, "If you try to impress others with your periodic fasting, you better hope that people applaud because their temporary affirmation is all you're gonna get. But, if you keep your fasting between you and your Heavenly Father, you will earn a reward in Heaven that will last for eternity." Think about that the next time you try to impress someone with your spiritual activities.

Closing Thought

You may need to tell a few family members and friends when you fast. Otherwise, they may pester you about not eating. However, be very careful that you aren't trying to impress them when you tell them. Don't ruin a good activity with a bad motive.

Journal

Day 26

THERE'S SO MUCH MORE TO THE CHRISTIAN LIFE!

Pastor Matt Ellis

First Baptist Church of Polk City, Florida

I sang in a southern Gospel quartet when I was a student at a Christian college. We sang in churches all across Kentucky, Ohio, and as far north as Michigan. Those years about killed my spiritual life. On so many Sundays, I was immersed in dead church experiences. The body was dead; it just hadn't stopped twitching.

And as I quietly stood in judgment over those people, I realized that I did not have the joy of the Lord in my heart, either. I remember thinking, "There's GOT to be more to the Christian life than this!"

God, in His grace, led me to purchase A. W. Tozer's book, *The Pursuit of God*. My spiritual eyes began to open. I observed that God created me for Himself. When He saved me, He invited me into a love relationship with Him to enjoy Him to my heart's content.

I eventually purchased and devoured John Piper's book, *Desiring God*. As this book pointed me to so many familiar Scriptures, I saw that there was much more happiness intended for every Jesus-follower than I had been experiencing.

I began to look at verses like Exodus 33:18 in a new way:

"Then Moses said, 'Please, let me see your glory.'"
Exodus 33:18 (CSB)

I realized Moses wasn't asking for a dry, boring religious experience. Instead, he was like a kid with his face plastered to a candy store's front window, pleading with the owner to open the door.

Closing Thought

Maybe your eyes are dry; your heart is cold; and you suspect there is more to the Christian life than your present experience. There is! God is inviting you into a loving relationship with Him. Spend time in prayer, sharing your desire to experience His glorious presence. And then look for ways He will reveal Himself to you, especially in His Word . . . and never stop craving more of Him!

Journal

Day 27

THIRSTY FOR GOD

Pastor Matt Ellis
First Baptist Church of Polk City, Florida

We know we should pursue God. We know we should find our delight in Him. Yet, if you are like me, we tend to settle into a lifeless, predictable spiritual existence when life is easy. The hard truth is that we sometimes don't chase after God until life gets hard.

Our prayer time and Bible intake often take a hit when life is easy. These spiritual disciplines become lifeless and dull. Yet, when something terrible happens, our hearts crave to grab hold of our God again.

"As a deer longs for flowing streams, so I long for you, God.
I thirst for God, the living God. When can I come and appear before God?
My tears have been my food day and night,
while all day long people say to me, 'Where is your God?'
I remember this as I pour out my heart: how I walked with many,
leading the festive procession to the house of God,
with joyful and thankful shouts.
Why, my soul, are you so dejected? Why are you in such turmoil?
Put your hope in God, for I will still praise him, my Savior and my God.
I am deeply depressed;

therefore I remember you from the land of Jordan
and the peaks of Hermon, from Mount Mizar.
Deep calls to deep in the roar of your waterfalls;
all your breakers and your billows have swept over me.
The LORD will send his faithful love by day;
his song will be with me in the night—a prayer to the God of my life.
I will say to God, my rock, 'Why have you forgotten me?
Why must I go about in sorrow because of the enemy's oppression?'
My adversaries taunt me, as if crushing my bones,
while all day long they say to me, 'Where is your God?'
Why, my soul, are you so dejected? Why are you in such turmoil?
Put your hope in God, for I will still praise him, my Savior and my God."
Psalm 42 (CSB)

As we read Psalm 42, we observe that the psalmist was struggling. He was going through difficult times, and his enemies were taunting him. To make matters worse, he held God somewhat responsible and wondered why He wasn't coming to help.

But the psalmist wasn't content to wallow in fear and discouragement. He knew that God wasn't the one who left. Instead, he recognized that he was the one who wandered from a joy-filled relationship with his God.

So, as he struggled with his current condition, he determined to chase after God and began this psalm with a very picturesque analogy. Just as a dehydrated deer is consumed with nothing else besides satisfying its thirst, the psalmist was just as consumed with satisfying his soul's thirsty longing with an enjoyable relationship with God.

While we don't like it when life gets difficult, it is usually those times that give us the incentive to realign our spiritual priorities. Those unenviable circumstances allow us to realize that our hearts are not enjoying our God. In those moments, we can determine, by God's grace, to renew our pursuit of Him.

Closing Thought

Are you desiring God to the same extent that a deer with a parched tongue desires to satisfy its thirst? If not, then realize that the difficulties you may be experiencing are, among other things, an opportunity to renew your desire for and motivate you to chase after and enjoy your God. Write down some difficulties you are facing right now; and then, after some reflection, write down some ways that they can motivate you to chase after and enjoy God again.

Journal

Day 28

"GOD, PLEASE BRING REVIVAL AGAIN!"

Pastor Matt Ellis
First Baptist Church of Polk City, Florida

When you look back over your life, can you identify some times when you enjoyed the Lord? Are there special moments when you clearly sensed God's forgiveness and cleansing? Are there times when the Lord moved in your life and turned your anxiety, sadness, or fear into joy?

That's what we observe in Psalm 85:1-3:

"Lord, you showed favor to your land; you restored the fortunes of Jacob.
You forgave your people's guilt; you covered all their sin. *Selah.*
You withdrew all your fury; you turned from your burning anger."
Psalm 85:1-3 (CSB)

The writer looked in the rearview mirror of his life and recognized that there were times when God moved powerfully among His people. He rescued them and turned their sadness into happiness in Him.

And then we get to Psalm 85:4-7:

"Return to us, God of our salvation,
and abandon your displeasure with us.
Will you be angry with us forever?

Will you prolong your anger for all generations?
Will you not revive us again so that your people may rejoice in you?
Show us your faithful love, LORD, and give us your salvation."
Psalm 85:4-7 (CSB)

We realize that the psalmist was in trouble again. God's people had sinned, and the Lord seemed angry with them. God was disciplining His people, and the psalmist pleaded with Him to help and restore them.

Have you experienced seasons when God seemed so far away and you lost your happiness in Him? Did you feel that the difficulties in your life were God's discipline for your disobedience?

What do we do in times like these? We do what the psalmist did! We pray, acknowledge our sins, and seek to be revived. Revived simply means being brought alive again so we can enjoy the Lord's presence and favor.

Friend, the problems you are presently going through could be a blessing in disguise. We typically don't chase after God when life is good. It is when life gets challenging that we are motivated to seek to alleviate the pain. For the Christian, the answer always includes chasing after God.

Closing Thought

If you sense that your sinful choices have brought about a time of trouble, spend today (or longer) fasting and praying. Acknowledge and turn from your sin. Seek the Lord, asking Him to restore you to the enjoyment you once had in Him.

Journal

Day 29

FAST WITH COMPASSION

Pastor Drew White
Faith Baptist Church of Lakeland, Florida

**"Wherefore have we fasted, say they, and thou seest not?
wherefore have we afflicted our soul, and thou takest no knowledge?
Behold, in the day of your fast ye find pleasure,
and exact all your labours.
Behold, ye fast for strife and debate,
and to smite with the fist of wickedness:
ye shall not fast as ye do this day, to make your voice to be heard on high.
Is it such a fast that I have chosen? a day for a man to afflict his soul?
is it to bow down his head as a bulrush,
and to spread sackcloth and ashes under him?
wilt thou call this a fast, and an acceptable day to the Lord?
Is not this the fast that I have chosen? to loose the bands of wickedness,
to undo the heavy burdens, and to let the oppressed go free,
and that ye break every yoke?
Is it not to deal thy bread to the hungry,
and that thou bring the poor that are cast out to thy house?
when thou seest the naked, that thou cover him;
and that thou hide not thyself from thine own flesh?"
Isaiah 58:3-7 (KJV)**

In the midst of our spiritual pursuits, it's easy to lose sight of what truly matters to God. In Isaiah 58, the Lord addresses a people who had been observing religious practices, including fasting, yet their hearts were far from Him. Their fasts had become ritualistic, devoid of genuine compassion and concern for others.

God calls attention to the essence of true fasting, a spiritual discipline that extends beyond mere abstaining from food. The essence of true fasting lies in our willingness to alleviate the suffering of others. It's not about impressing God with our piety but about living out His heart for justice, mercy, and love. God's desire is not just for us to deny ourselves physical sustenance but also to loosen the chains of injustice, lift heavy burdens from the oppressed, and break the yokes that bind people.

Prayer: Dear Heavenly Father, teach us to fast with a heart of compassion. May our acts of self-denial align with Your desire for justice and mercy. Show us how to break the chains of oppression and share Your love with those in need. Let our lives be a reflection of Your grace. In Jesus' name, amen.

Action Step

Today, take a moment to reflect on the ways you can make a tangible difference in the lives of those around you. Seek out opportunities to lend a hand to those burdened by life's challenges. Extend a hand of friendship to the lonely; offer sustenance to the hungry; and clothe the needy. Let your actions be a manifestation of God's love.

Journal

Day 30

IN OUR WEAKNESS, THE SPIRIT INTERCEDES

Pastor Drew White
Faith Baptist Church of Lakeland, Florida

Life often confronts us with challenges that leave us feeling helpless and overwhelmed. We grapple with sickness, uncertainty, and heartache, unsure of how to express our deepest feelings to God. In these moments of weakness, the Apostle Paul reminds us in Romans 8:26 that we have a divine Helper: the Holy Spirit.

**"Likewise the Spirit also helpeth our infirmities:
for we know not what we should pray for as we ought:
but the Spirit itself maketh intercession for us with groanings
which cannot be uttered.
And he that searcheth the hearts knoweth what is the mind of the Spirit,
because he maketh intercession for the saints according to the will of God."
Romans 8:26-27 (KJV)**

The Holy Spirit knows the depths of our hearts and the burdens we carry even when we lack the words to express them. He steps in, interceding on our behalf with wordless groanings that transcend our finite understanding. Our inadequacy in prayer becomes a bridge to divine communication as the Spirit bridges the gap between our hearts and the heart of God.

This passage teaches us that God not only *invites* us but also *expects* us to come to Him in our times of need even when our words fail us. Rather than fretting over how our prayers may sound, we can lean into vulnerability, trusting that the Spirit's intercession aligns our prayers with God's perfect will.

Prayer: Dear Heavenly Father, thank You for the gift of the Holy Spirit who intercedes for us in our times of weakness. Help us to approach You with honesty and vulnerability, knowing that You understand even our unspoken needs. May we find comfort in the assurance that You work all things together for our good. In Jesus' name, amen.

Action Step

Next time you find yourself at a loss for words in prayer, remember that the Holy Spirit is ready to intercede for you. Offer your heart's concerns to God even if they can't be expressed in words (silence can be okay). Embrace the comfort of His presence, and trust that He understands your unspoken needs.

Journal

Day 31

A CALL TO REVIVAL: RESTORING HEARTS AND NATIONS

Pastor Drew White
Faith Baptist Church of Lakeland, Florida

In a world filled with distractions, chaos, and brokenness, the call to revival resonates as a beacon of hope. In 2 Chronicles 7:14 God provides a timeless blueprint for revival, a spiritual awakening that begins with His people. The verse outlines four essential steps that pave the way for personal and national restoration.

"If my people, which are called by my name, shall humble themselves,
and pray, and seek my face, and turn from their wicked ways;
then will I hear from heaven,
and will forgive their sin, and will heal their land."
II Chronicles 7:14 (KJV)

Humble ourselves: Revival starts with humility. Recognizing our limitations and acknowledging our dependence on God, we humble ourselves before His greatness. We shed the pride that distances us from His grace and open ourselves to His transforming power.

Pray and seek His face: Prayer is the lifeline of revival. It's through prayer that we align our hearts with God's will, seeking His guidance and presence. Revival isn't a formula; it's a relationship.

As we draw near to God in prayer, we experience His closeness and discover the depth of His love.

Turn from our wicked ways: True revival demands repentance. We must turn away from our sinful paths, forsaking all that separates us from God. Repentance isn't just a change of behavior but a change of heart, a sincere desire to live in alignment with God's truth and righteousness.

God's promise of healing: When we follow these steps, God responds with a promise. He assures us that He will hear our cries, forgive our sins, and bring healing to our lives and our land. Revival is not a distant dream; it's a reality within reach. Revival is not just personal; it has the power to transform societies and nations. It begins with us, the people called by God's name. As we embrace humility, prayer, repentance, and God's promises, we invite His transformative power into our lives and witness the healing of our hearts and our world.

Prayer: Heavenly Father, ignite within us a passion for revival. Help us to humble ourselves, draw near to You in prayer, and turn away from anything that hinders our relationship with You. We long for Your healing touch in our lives and in our land. May revival start in our hearts and spread like wildfire, bringing glory to Your name. In Jesus' name we pray, amen.

Action Step

Right now, reflect on your life in light of 2 Chronicles 7:14. Humble yourself; spend quality time in prayer, seeking God's presence; examine your heart for any wicked ways; and make a deliberate commitment to turn away from them.

Journal

Day 32

A HEART RENEWED FOR REVIVAL

Pastor Drew White
Faith Baptist Church of Lakeland, Florida

Revival is not just an event; it's a transformational journey that starts within the depths of our hearts. In Psalm 51, we find David's heartfelt plea to God after his grievous sin with Bathsheba. His brokenness and repentance serve as a profound example of the posture we must adopt for revival to take place in our lives.

"Create in me a clean heart, O God; and renew a right spirit within me."
Psalm 51:10 (KJV)

Psalm 51:10 contains the essence of revival: a deep longing for God to create a clean heart within us and to renew a right spirit. This goes beyond mere external changes; it's about an inward transformation that aligns our desires, motives, and attitudes with God's will.

Revival begins with recognizing the need for a heart transformation. Just as a garden needs to be tilled, we must allow God to till the soil of our hearts, breaking up the hardness and removing the weeds of sin and selfishness. This process can be painful as we confront our shortcomings and surrender our will to God's refining fire.

Prayer: Heavenly Father, create in me a clean heart and renew a right spirit within me. I long for true revival not just in my actions, but also in the depths of my being. Help me embrace the pruning process, knowing that Your love guides every cut. May my life be a testament to Your transformative power. In Jesus' name, amen.

Action Step

Today, take time for self-analysis and prayer. Ask the Holy Spirit to reveal areas of your heart that need cleansing and renewal. Write down specific attitudes, habits, or sins that you want God to transform. Remember, revival starts with honesty and humility before God. As you journey towards revival, remember that God's grace is sufficient for your weaknesses. A heart renewed by God's love and grace is the foundation upon which genuine revival is built. Allow His Spirit to work within you, transforming you from the inside out; and watch as He brings forth a beautiful garden of spiritual growth and renewed passion for Him.

Journal

Day 33

LOOKING AT THE WRONG PERSON

Dr. Lito Lucas
Philippine International Christian Fellowship of Lakeland, Florida

"I will raise my eyes to the mountains;
From where will my help come?
My help *comes* from the LORD, Who made heaven and earth.
He will not allow your foot to slip;
He who watches over you will not slumber.
Behold, He who watches over Israel
Will neither slumber nor sleep.
The LORD is your protector;
The LORD is your shade on your right hand.
The sun will not beat down on you by day,
Nor the moon by night.
The LORD will protect you from all evil;
He will keep your soul.
The LORD will guard your going out
and your coming in From this time and forever."
Psalm 121 (NASB)

Psalm 121 is one of the pilgrimage songs. As the pilgrims traveled to Jerusalem to worship the Lord, they sang this song to express their confidence that the Lord would protect them from dangerous elements. They never placed their trust in something or someone else to protect them. The pilgrims knew that help came only from the Maker of Heaven and earth. They confidently trusted God's divine protection because the Lord never sleeps nor slumbers. He watched them at all times.

How about you? When fears or worries grip your heart, where do you look for help? Your life's journey may not be easy right now, and it wears you down physically, emotionally, and spiritually. Instead of looking for help from someone else, why not ask first the sovereign God to help you? Place your trust in the Lord who created everything out of nothing. Why? For He knows the ins and outs of your life. He knows your situation, and He will help and guide you to navigate your fears and worries.

The psalmist said in verse 8:

"The Lord will keep your going out and your coming in from this time forth and forevermore."
Psalm 121:8 (NASB)

The psalmist assures you that in any situation you can trust the Lord. If God created everything, how much more can He provide all the help you need during your difficult time? Avoid placing your trust in the wrong person. Instead, place your trust in the One who loves you and cares for you.

Prayer

Lord, help me overcome all my worries and fears. I may not understand everything that is going on in my life, but I know I can trust You that You will guide and keep me always in Your loving care. In Jesus' name, amen.

Journal

Day 34

ASKING FOR THE RIGHT THING

Dr. Lito Lucas
Philippine International Christian Fellowship of Lakeland, Florida

"If you remain in me and my words remain in you, ask whatever you want and it will be done for you." John 15:7 (CSB)

When we pray, it does not mean that God will answer our prayer right away. Our verse does not say that whatever we ask God for He will immediately give us. Sadly, we sometimes treat prayer like a microwave or a vending machine: we want an instant answer to our prayer.

God does not work that way. He does not give in to what we want. We cannot demand or coerce God to answer our prayer the way we want it. Sometimes, we feel entitled to get what we ask from God because we did or are doing something for God like giving our tithes or being active in church. We cannot bribe God.

The key to answered prayer is based on trusting who Christ is and letting His Word permeate our life. If we do that, we will not ask anything that is outside His nature and His will. The more we get into God's Word, the more it will condition and align our mind to His mind.

Perhaps, our prayers are not being heard because we are not allowing God's Word to saturate our mind. If we want to know someone personally, we will invest time to get to know that person well. Likewise with God. When we invest time praying to Him and reading His Word, we will know His will, and we will pray for the right thing.

Prayer

Lord, help me to know You more so I can ask for things that You want me to do or have and not for what I want to do or have. In Jesus' name, amen.

Journal

Day 35

GOD KNOWS BEST

Dr. Lito Lucas
Philippine International Christian Fellowship of Lakeland, Florida

The Apostle Paul personally encountered Christ on his way to Damascus to persecute Jesus' followers. After his conversion experience, he became a staunch defender of the church and the Christian faith. Inspired by the Holy Spirit, he wrote almost half of the New Testament.

"... especially because of the extraordinary revelations.
Therefore, so that I would not exalt myself,
a thorn in the flesh was given to me,
a messenger of Satan to torment me so that I would not exalt myself.
Concerning this,
I pleaded with the Lord three times that it would leave me.
But he said to me, 'My grace is sufficient for you,
for my power is perfected in weakness.'
Therefore, I will most gladly boast all the more about my weaknesses,
so that Christ's power may reside in me.
So I take pleasure in weaknesses, insults, hardships,
persecutions, and in difficulties, for the sake of Christ.
For when I am weak, then I am strong."
2 Corinthians 12:7-10 (CSB)

Even though he was a faithful follower of Christ, Paul was not exempt from trials and suffering.

In our passage, he asked the Lord three times to remove his "thorn in the flesh." No one really knows Paul's physical affliction, but he dealt with it while doing the Lord's work. He prayed for healing, but God answered him differently. He answered Paul's prayer but not the way Paul wanted.

God says in verse 9,

"My grace is sufficient for you, for my power is perfected in weakness."
2 Corinthians 12:9 (CSB)

What does this mean? It means that God gave Paul grace to endure his afflictions, to keep him humble, to demonstrate God's power in his life, and to find strength in Christ when he was weak. These made Paul strong in the faith so his testimony gave glory to God.

Perhaps you are suffering right now and are asking the Lord to heal or help you to overcome your difficult situation. Despite this, it may seem like the Lord is not answering your prayer. Sometimes, His answer is different . . . but He knows what is good for you.

Did Paul complain? Of course not! He trusted the Lord, knowing His answer was better than what he asked for. Likewise, when God does not answer your prayer the way you want Him to, He knows what is good for you. You just need to trust Him. Do not doubt His plan. It is better than yours.

Prayer

Lord, I commit to You my problem. I trust that You have a better plan for me, so I thank You. In Jesus' name, amen.

Journal

Day 36

DELIGHT IN THE LORD

Dr. Lito Lucas
Philippine International Christian Fellowship of Lakeland, Florida

The psalmist encouraged the people not to be envious of sinful people and their prosperity because it would be short-lived. Instead, they should trust the Lord who answers the prayer of His people.

"Take delight in the LORD, and he will give you your heart's desires. Commit your way to the LORD; trust in him, and he will act."
Psalm 37:4-5 (CSB)

However, there is a caveat here: God does not just answer our prayer. Two important words must be noted in our passage: delight and commit.

"Delight" means to refresh oneself. Refreshing oneself in the Lord is to renew or to revive a close fellowship with Him. To delight in the Lord is to enrich your fellowship with Him.

How do you do that? You spend time in His Word. Knowing Him intimately develops and strengthens your faith. Knowing Him helps you to pray in line with His will, and He will reward you when you delight in Him.

Also, *commit* everything to Him. "Commit" means to turn over oneself to God. You trust the outcome to Him. You give everything to Him that concerns you and let Him take care of it. You trust His promises in His Word.

To delight in the Lord and to commit your life to Him are essential to answered prayer. God will not give you the desires of your heart if you are not delighting in Him and not committing your life to Him.

So, if you want your prayers to be heard, desire God. Do not be envious of the prosperity of the non-believers. Their pleasures will not last long, but delighting in your fellowship with the Lord and committing everything to Him will have the outcome of God's blessing that will last for a lifetime.

Prayer

Lord, I want to know You more. I commit my life to You, and I trust You that You will take care of all my concerns. In Jesus' name, amen.

Journal

Day 37

DO NOT LOSE HEART

Pastor Greg Wilkerson
First Baptist Church of Mulberry, Florida

Do you ever feel like giving up? Do you ever think your prayers do not matter? Have you ever wondered if God even cares?

**"And he told them a parable to the effect that they ought always to pray and not lose heart.
He said, 'In a certain city there was a judge who neither feared God nor respected man.
And there was a widow in that city who kept coming to him and saying, "Give me justice against my adversary."
For a while he refused, but afterward he said to himself, "Though I neither fear God nor respect man,
yet because this widow keeps bothering me, I will give her justice,
so that she will not beat me down by her continual coming."'
And the Lord said, 'Hear what the unrighteous judge says.
And will not God give justice to his elect, who cry to him day and night?
Will he delay long over them?
I tell you, he will give justice to them speedily.
Nevertheless, when the Son of Man comes, will he find faith on earth?'"
Luke 18:1-8 (ESV)**

In Luke 18:1-8, Jesus shares a parable about a persistent widow who continuously went to a wicked judge looking for justice. Before diving too deeply into the parable, it is important to pay attention to verse 1, for in this verse is given the reason for the parable of the persistent widow, which is that we should always pray and not lose heart.

The wicked judge in the parable has no fear of God and no respect for others. However, he answers the widow's request and provides justice for her. It was not because he cared about her or her situation; he simply was tired of her endlessly bothering him.

We must remember that God is unlike the wicked judge. God *does* care about us. God cares about our situations in life. God is never bothered by our coming to Him. As a matter of fact, He always wants us to continuously come to Him. God hears your prayers, and He cares.

So, do not lose heart. Do not give up. Know that your prayer matters. God really does cares. Keep praying and trusting God.

Action Step

Identify something that you have stopped praying about due to discouragement. Resume praying about it today. Remember always to pray, and do not lose heart.

Journal

Day 38

ACCESS

Pastor Greg Wilkerson
First Baptist Church of Mulberry, Florida

If you are anything like me, then you have a ton of keys. Have you ever thought of the significance of having a key? The possession of a key gives a person unlimited access to something. I have a key to my parents' house, which gives me the privilege of having access to enter their home whenever I would like. Not everyone has this access because not everyone has a key.

"Since then we have a great high priest
who has passed through the heavens, Jesus, the Son of God,
let us hold fast our confession.
For we do not have a high priest
who is unable to sympathize with our weaknesses,
but one who in every respect has been tempted as we are,
yet without sin.
Let us then with confidence draw near to the throne of grace,
that we may receive mercy and find grace to help in time of need."
Hebrews 4:14-16 (ESV)

Hebrews 4:14 tells us that in Jesus we have a high priest.

"Since then we have a great high priest who has passed through the heavens, Jesus, the Son of God, let us hold fast our confession."
Hebrews 4:14 (ESV)

Jesus is not just a high priest, but He is also able to sympathize with our weakness. Jesus understands the pressures of this life. He faced temptation just like we do. The difference is Jesus never sinned, which makes him the perfect high priest.

The job of the high priest was to be a mediator between God and the people. God would come in judgment because of the sins of the people; and the high priest would stand in their place, offering sacrifices that satisfied God's justice and demonstrated His mercy by punishing an innocent animal in place of a guilty human being.

Jesus fulfills both the role of the sacrifice and the high priest for us, which in turn allows us access to the throne of grace. Hebrews 4:16 states that with confidence we can draw near to the throne of grace.

"Let us then with confidence draw near to the throne of grace, that we may receive mercy and find grace to help in time of need."
Hebrews 4:16 (ESV)

This access is available to us at any time of need. At the throne of grace, we can receive mercy and grace.

Action Step

Start praying today for a specific request, having confidence in approaching God in your time of need. Jesus is the key that grants you access to the throne of grace.

Journal

Day 39

PRIORITIES DETERMINE OUTCOME

Pastor Greg Wilkerson
First Baptist Church of Mulberry, Florida

Have you ever noticed that the things we prioritize get accomplished? What are your top priorities in life? Sometimes we are guilty of saying something is a priority, but our actions and outcomes reveal otherwise. Individuals and churches can claim that they would like to experience revival, but their actions will reveal whether revival is truly a top priority.

What is a requirement for revival to be a top priority?

"But seek first the kingdom of God and his righteousness, and all these things will be added to you."
Matthew 6:33 (ESV)

Even though Matthew 6:33 does not speak about revival, it does speak about priorities. Our top priority must be to seek the kingdom of God and His righteousness above all else.

Matthew 6:33 is part of a longer passage that deals with worrying about the things we need in life such as food, drink, clothing, etc.

"Therefore I tell you, do not be anxious about your life,
what you will eat or what you will drink, nor about your body,
what you will put on.
Is not life more than food, and the body more than clothing?
Look at the birds of the air: they neither sow nor reap nor gather into barns,
and yet your heavenly Father feeds them.
Are you not of more value than they?
And which of you by being anxious can add a single hour
to his span of life?
And why are you anxious about clothing?
Consider the lilies of the field, how they grow:
they neither toil nor spin,
yet I tell you, even Solomon in all his glory
was not arrayed like one of these.
But if God so clothes the grass of the field,
which today is alive and tomorrow is thrown into the oven,
will he not much more clothe you, O you of little faith?
Therefore do not be anxious, saying, 'What shall we eat?'
or 'What shall we drink?' or 'What shall we wear?'
For the Gentiles seek after all these things,
and your heavenly Father knows that you need them all.
But seek first the kingdom of God and his righteousness,
and all these things will be added to you.
Therefore do not be anxious about tomorrow,
for tomorrow will be anxious for itself.
Sufficient for the day is its own trouble."
Matthew 6:25-34 (ESV)

The Scripture is not denying that we *need* these things; but rather than *worrying* about these things, our focus and priority needs to be on seeking God first.

There are endless amounts of excellent sermons and books that cover the different aspects of revival from repentance to worship. We can become guilty of focusing—and even worrying—so much on the details of revival that we forget that the priority is to seek the kingdom of God and His righteousness first.

Action Step

Identify your top priority in life by recognizing your actions and outcomes. Is seeking God really your top priority? If not, ask God to help you set your priorities in order.

Journal

Day 40

GOD HAS A PLAN FOR YOU

Pastor Greg Wilkerson
First Baptist Church of Mulberry, Florida

Jeremiah 29:11 is a popular verse and is often used to encourage others about what the future may hold.

"For I know the plans I have for you, declares the Lord, plans for welfare and not for evil, to give you a future and a hope." Jeremiah 29:11 (ESV)

We like to read this verse with the idea that God's plan for us is to be prosperous and successful. Is that really God's plan for us? To understand God's plan for us we must first identify to whom God is speaking in this verse.

God is speaking through the prophet Jeremiah to all the people whom Nebuchadnezzar had taken into exile from Jerusalem to Babylon. This letter to the exiles was instructions on how they should not forsake their relationship with God. It was meant to provide them hope in a time where it seemed all hope had been lost.

Secondly, to understand God's plan for us we must pay careful attention to the verses that follow verse 11.

"Then you will call upon me and come and pray to me,
and I will hear you.
You will seek me and find me, when you seek me with all your heart."
Jeremiah 29:12-13 (ESV)

In verses 12-13, several words stand out: "*call upon me,*" "*come and pray to me,*" and "*seek me.*" God is calling on the exiles to seek Him and to pray to Him. Notice what God promises that He will do when the exiles follow His instructions: God promises that He will hear their prayers, that they will find Him, and that He will bring them back from exile.

God does have a plan for us today, but that plan is not for us to be prosperous and successful according to the world's standard. God's plan is to restore His people to a right relationship with Himself. God's plan is for His people to seek Him with their whole heart and to have a genuine prayer life.

Action Step

Are you seeking a prosperous and successful life according to the world's standard or are you seeking God with your whole heart? Find some time today to seek God and to call to Him in prayer.

Journal

FINAL THOUGHTS

Dr. Richard Williamson

Central Florida Baptist Association

Forty days is an important period of time in the Bible. It is how long it rained during the flood (Genesis 7:12); it is how long Moses was on the mountain receiving the Ten Commandments (Exodus 34:28); it is how long the spies explored the promised land (Numbers 13:25); it is how long Jesus appeared to his disciples after his death (Acts 1:3); and it is how long Jesus prayed and fasted during his temptation just after his baptism (Matthew 4:2, Mark 1:13).

Forty days is a lengthy time . . . lengthy enough for real spiritual progress. Spiritually important things can take place over a period of 40 days. It is our hope that these 40 days have seen significant spiritual encouragement and growth in your life.

It is our prayer that this time has just been the beginning. Keep praying; keep fasting; keep seeking revival. Focus on bringing about revival in your own heart by utilizing the great power of prayer, praying for what really matters; developing a greater hunger and thirst for God; and learning to delight in our Lord Jesus Christ.

Made in the USA
Columbia, SC
30 June 2025